TOWERS

IN THE

NORTH

THE BROCHS OF SCOTLAND

TOWERS
IN THE
NORTH
THE BROCHS OF SCOTLAND

IAN ARMIT

TEMPUS

First published 2003

PUBLISHED IN THE UNITED KINGDOM BY:
Tempus Publishing Ltd
The Mill, Brimscombe Port
Stroud, Gloucestershire GL5 2QG

PUBLISHED IN THE UNITED STATES OF AMERICA BY:
Tempus Publishing Inc.
2 Cumberland Street
Charleston, SC 29401

British Library Cataloguing in Publication Data.
A catalogue record for this book is available from the British Library.

ISBN 0 7524 1932 3

Typesetting and origination by Tempus Publishing.
Printed in Great Britain by Midway Colour Print, Wiltshire.

CONTENTS

For my daughter Rowan

ACKNOWLEDGEMENTS

The author and publisher would like to thank the following for permission to reproduce illustrations: Historic Scotland (figures **2**, **9**, **11**, **12**, **14**, **26**, **27**, **36**, **51**, **52**, and **colour plates 1**, **2**, **4**, **6-8**, **10**, **11**, **13**, **14**, **17**, **22**, **23**), Museum nan Eilean (figure **30**), the Royal Commission on the Ancient and Historical Monuments of Scotland (figures **3**, **5**, **13**, **15**, **32** & **48**), and Professor Dennis Harding (figures **20**, **21**, **25**, **35** & **45**). Illustrations **11**, **12**, **30** and **36** were drawn by Alan Braby and other original illustrations by Libby Mulqueeny. The reconstruction drawing of Clickhimin (**9**) is by Alan Sorrell.

I would like to thank Professor David Breeze in particular for his assistance with the illustrations. Conversations with numerous friends and colleagues over the years have helped form my views on the whole range of subjects covered in this book: the work of many of these individuals is represented in the 'Further reading' section at the end of the book. I would also like to thank Andrew Dunwell and Catriona Leask for their comments on earlier drafts of various sections. Finally I must thank Peter Kemmis Betty and all at Tempus for their extraordinary patience.

LIST OF COLOUR PLATES

LIST OF ILLUSTRATIONS

1

THE BROCH HUNTERS

In late September 1773, Dr Samuel Johnson and his travelling companion, James Boswell, were taken to visit Dun Beag, near Struan in Skye. Their host, a certain Mr Macqueen, speculated that the ruin might be that of a 'Danish fort', although local opinion held that it had been the seat of the first Macleod chiefs. Dr Johnson, according to the account in his *Journey to the Western Islands of Scotland*, thought it more likely to have been a cattle enclosure from more recent 'lawless times'. Dr Johnson's description of the outing, which also included visits to a souterrain and a natural sea-cave, reflects the growing fascination of the eighteenth-century intelligentsia with all things antiquarian and ancient, be they man-made or natural. It was from such beginnings that antiquarian interest in the broch towers of northern and western Scotland slowly began to take shape.

What is a 'broch'?

The word 'broch' derives from the Norse word 'borg' (meaning fort), which was probably first applied to these ruined structures by Viking raiders during the ninth century AD. Various derivatives of the original word ('brough', 'borough', 'borve' etc.) have since been applied promiscuously throughout Atlantic Scotland to a whole range of man-made and natural places. Archaeologists adopted the standardised spelling 'broch' in the late nineteenth century to describe a specific group of prehistoric drystone roundhouses with a range of architectural features such as internal stairs and galleries. The newly defined class of monument was best represented by those astonishing survivals from antiquity, Mousa in Shetland, Dun Carloway in Lewis, Dun Dornaigil in Sutherland, and Duns Troddan and Telve in Glenelg, the archetypal broch towers of the north and west (**1**).

Few prehistoric monuments are more immediately evocative than the broch towers. Their grim, outwardly featureless stone shells can be found scattered across the fragmented landscapes of the Highlands and Islands, often

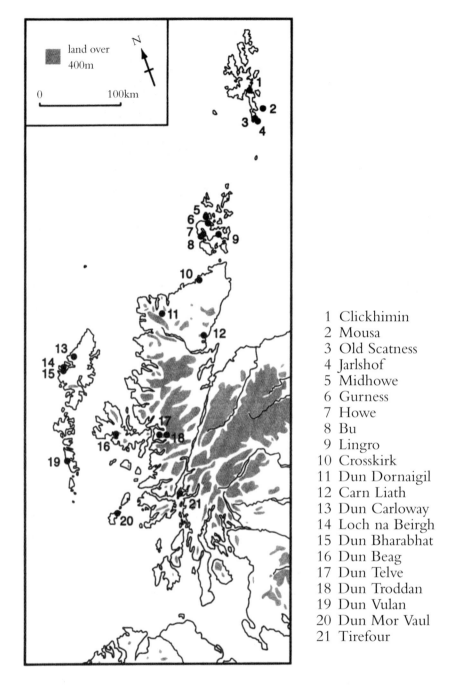

land over 400m

N

0   100km

1 Clickhimin
2 Mousa
3 Old Scatness
4 Jarlshof
5 Midhowe
6 Gurness
7 Howe
8 Bu
9 Lingro
10 Crosskirk
11 Dun Dornaigil
12 Carn Liath
13 Dun Carloway
14 Loch na Beirgh
15 Dun Bharabhat
16 Dun Beag
17 Dun Telve
18 Dun Troddan
19 Dun Vulan
20 Dun Mor Vaul
21 Tirefour

1 *Map of Atlantic Scotland and adjacent areas showing the location of some of the main sites mentioned in the text*

2   *The broch tower of Mousa, Shetland*

formidably perched on rugged outcrops or inaccessible islets (**colour plates 1** & **3**). The handful of spectacularly well-preserved examples, such as Mousa (**2** & **colour plate 2**), are among the best prehistoric buildings in Europe. The tall stone walls, the winding stairs, and the architectural intricacies of scarcement and wall void, challenge each visitor to form their own interpretation of how these buildings would once have functioned. With such raw material to work from, it is no surprise that broch towers have inspired a long and tangled tradition of debate and dissension.

Agreeing a proper working definition for brochs has never been straight-forward. There are many hundreds of ruinous drystone roundhouses scattered around the north and west of Scotland. Over the centuries the stone from these buildings has been robbed away to build later houses, field walls and the other stone structures that make up the modern landscape (**3**). Very occasionally the superstructure survives well enough to show that these were once immensely tall buildings of sophisticated design – in other words, broch towers. Yet for every Mousa or Dun Telve, there are tens or hundreds of dilapidated ruins where we have simply no way of knowing what the original superstructure was like. This problem of preservation is at the root of some of the deepest and most long-running disputes between archaeologists involved in studying brochs.

3 *An early view of Dun Carloway, Lewis, showing the presence of nineteenth-century blackhouses. Much of the stone from the broch tower may have been robbed out to build these structures*

For some archaeologists, the term broch can be usefully applied only to those structures exhibiting key architectural features, most importantly a high, hollow wall containing superimposed galleries. Such a definition will obviously exclude any building that does not survive to sufficient height to display such features. Thus the numbers of accepted brochs may be kept artificially low. This may not seem terribly important at first glance, but it can have a distorting effect on the way that these buildings, and thus the communities which built them, are perceived. For example, if we believe that there were only ever a small number of broch towers, then we might interpret them as the fortified castles of a social élite; an Iron Age aristocracy. By contrast, if we accept that there may originally have been many hundreds that simply do not survive particularly well today, then such interpretations become unrealistic.

So how many brochs are there? Joseph Anderson, writing in the late nineteenth century estimated that there were around 370 brochs in Scotland, while later estimates increased the figure to around 500. Yet by 1965, the ever more rigorous definitions employed by archaeologists such as Euan MacKie had reduced the number of definite brochs to 104. A strict application of the architectural criteria could produce a much lower figure still. The question of course is an entirely artificial one, the answer depending entirely on how the definition of a broch is framed.

In recent years it has become increasingly apparent that the classic broch tower lies at one end of a spectrum of complexity, the other end being represented by the simple, low-walled roundhouse. Between these extremes lies a wide range of roundhouse forms, with varying degrees of architectural elaboration. Taken as a whole, this wider group of Atlantic roundhouses seems to date from around 700 BC through to around the end of the first millennium BC (**4**). In chapter 2 we will see how the building of the classic broch towers may be understood as a particularly remarkable architectural episode within this rather broader Atlantic roundhouse tradition.

Antiquarian beginnings

Quite when, where, and by whom the first broch was excavated we will probably never know for sure. Some early accounts, such as Principal Gordon's 1792 journal of his trip to Orkney, refer cryptically to earlier excavations of 'Danish' or 'Pictish' forts. There is little to suggest now, however, what scale of operations might have been involved. By the 1820s, however, sporadic assaults were being made on broch sites in Orkney in common with a wide range of the more obvious and prominent archaeological sites across Britain and beyond. Some, such as the Broch of Burgar in Orkney, suffered from repeated clearance by successive generations of excavators whose activities

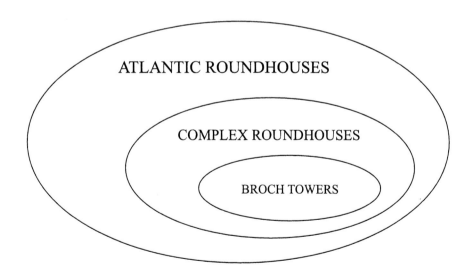

4 *The Atlantic roundhouse terminology used in this book. The term Atlantic roundhouse describes all of the massive-walled drystone roundhouses found in Atlantic Scotland, and contains a sub-set of more elaborate buildings known as complex roundhouses. As the diagram shows, broch towers are one specialised form of complex roundhouse. Complex roundhouses, as the name suggests, contain features such as intra-mural cells and stairs, but not all would have been tower-like buildings. Due to the vagaries of preservation it is impossible to know what proportion of complex roundhouses were originally broch towers*

removed what would nowadays be considered crucially important archaeological evidence. Unfortunately, the energetic but undisciplined howks of the eighteenth and early nineteenth centuries were seldom recorded beyond the most superficial level and did little to further understanding of these structures.

It was during the middle of the nineteenth century that the serious study of Scottish prehistory really began, and the prominence of brochs within the landscape ensured that they were at the forefront of archaeological attention. One of the figures from this period to have earned most respect from later archaeologists is Captain F.W.L. Thomas, a naval surveyor and antiquarian, who carried out detailed pioneering survey work in both Orkney and the Western Isles. His 1852 publication on the archaeological remains of Orkney commented on the 'Pictish Broughs', identifying them as dwellings distinct from the numerous (much earlier) burial mounds with which they had often been casually lumped in the past. Thomas' work included a call-to-arms for further excavation to elucidate these extraordinary structures, a call that was to be answered with great enthusiasm over succeeding decades.

In Orkney, the period from around 1850 to 1880 saw a huge upsurge of activity. Much of the early spade-work was carried out by an assortment of farmers, landowners and local clergy, but two individuals from the period stand out. James Farrer, the well-connected MP for Durham, developed a passionate interest in the Orkney brochs on his numerous visits to the islands. His enthusiasm was not, however, accompanied by any great methodological rigour, and his excavations, although extensive, could be chaotic. So much so, in fact, that John Hedges, in his history of Orcadian broch studies, describes him as 'a summer migrant who left a trail of destruction'. Posterity has been kinder to his contemporary and occasional collaborator, George Petrie, an Orcadian resident and estate factor, whose recording of his own excavations, and those of others, has preserved much information that would otherwise have been lost.

Through the efforts of these pioneers, the picture of a 'typical' northern broch site gradually came into focus. Petrie's excavations at Lingro in 1870 provided the first clear evidence for the presence of extensive clusters of outbuildings around certain broch sites (although until quite recently, such structures were seldom regarded as more than secondary squatter occupation of little intrinsic interest). A little later the first indications of stratified floor levels within brochs were reported, first by the Reverend Dr Traill at the Broch of Burrian (5), and then by W.G.T. Watt at the Broch of Borthwick, both in Orkney. Steadily a great mass of data was accumulated from which the first efforts at synthesis and interpretation could begin to be made.

This initial phase of fieldwork coincided with a period of transformation in perceptions of the prehistoric past. The establishment of the Three-Age system (the Stone, Bronze and Iron Ages), first published in English in 1848 by the Danish archaeologist C.J. Thomsen, enabled a new and systematic approach to

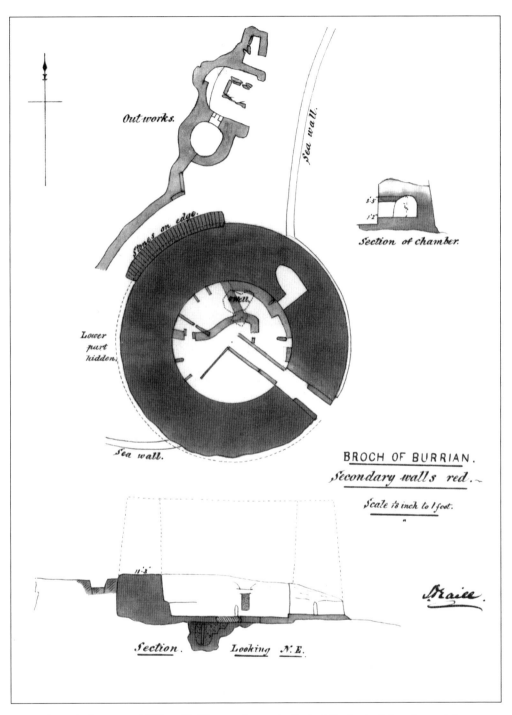

Out works.

Sea wall.

Section of chamber.

Stones on edge.

well.

Lower
part
hidden.

Sea wall.

BROCH OF BURRIAN.

Secondary walls red.

Scale ⅛ inch to 1 foot.

Section. Looking N.E.

5 *This early illustration of William Traill's excavations at the Broch of Burrian in Orkney is a typical product of the nineteenth century* the collection, cataloguing and interpretation of archaeological material. Across Europe, learned societies were being established and efforts made to produce 'national' prehistories often emphasising the importance and precociousness of particular peoples, races or regions. Scotland was particularly fortunate to have a succession of eminent archaeologists whose vision encompassed far more than parochial concerns. The first was Daniel Wilson, who coined the term 'prehistory' in his book of 1851, *Archaeology and Prehistoric Annals of Scotland*. Naturally, Wilson's book included a detailed discussion on brochs, at that time 'generally known as Burghs or Pictish-towers', which he saw as places of refuge for native communities threatened by the Viking onslaughts of the late first millennium AD. For the first time these structures were set in a wider context, as key elements in the construction of Scotland's prehistoric past.

By the mid-nineteenth century most Scottish antiquarians had, like Wilson, come to realise that brochs were essentially a native Scottish phenomenon, rather than the remains of intrusive Viking fortifications. Support for the 'nativist' position came from the distinguished Danish archaeologist, Jan Worsaae, who dismissed any links to Viking Age buildings in Scandinavia and asserted a 'Pictish or Celtic' origin for the brochs. Despite this, the controversy rumbled on through the century, providing fascinating insights into the rough and tumble of academic debate as the nascent discipline of archaeology emerged from the netherworld of antiquarian fancy. As late as 1877, James Fergusson was still arguing for a Norse origin, taking side-swipes at Worsaae, and grumbling about the imposition of the 'Danish system of the three ages' which had 'become the fashionable creed of this country [Scotland]'. 'According to it', he lamented, 'every building that cannot produce a written certificate of age, attested by contemporary witnesses, must belong to one of the three prehistoric ages.' Fergusson preferred to rely on the opinions of earlier (Scottish) luminaries such as Sir Walter Scott, whose muse had been stirred to visions of Viking earls and raiders on his visit to broch sites in Shetland. Fergusson could not accept that the 'Celts' as the 'older and inferior race' had been responsible for such impressive monuments, when their Norse conquerors had left so little of obvious note. The brochs, he declared, were patently 'the fortified nests of a race of sea-rovers'. Fergusson was already out-of-step with most of his contemporaries, however, as the finds accumulating from excavations in Orkney were by now clearly establishing a much earlier date.

Another myth dispelled around this time was the idea that the broch towers were related to the nuraghi – stone-built towers found in Sardinia. It is easy to see how this idea arose, since the nuraghi are tall, drystone conical towers with intra-mural stairs and super-imposed internal chambers. It gradually became apparent, however, that while the full flowering of broch architecture occurred around the end of the last millennium BC, the nuraghi flourished many centuries earlier, in the Sardinian Bronze Age. Added to this were many architectural dissimilarities, such as the vaulted roofing of the internal chambers of the Sardinian structures, which rather overshadowed the superficial impression of similarity. In many respects, however, the two architectural traditions may have evolved independently to serve similar social needs. Modern archaeological opinion tends to see the nuraghi as defensible farmsteads of prosperous land-holders, who displayed their social status and prestige through elaborate architecture. As we shall see, this is not dissimilar to current interpretations of brochs.

In the years following Wilson's publication, further efforts were made to synthesise the emerging evidence from excavations across Scotland. John Stuart's 1858 contribution to the *Proceedings of the Society of Antiquaries of Scotland* emphasised the distinctively Scottish character of the 'burghs' (Sir Henry Dryden writes in the same volume about the 'burg' of Mousa – terminology was still rather fluid). However, Stuart also drew comparisons with the Irish drystone forts such as the Grianan of Aileach, Co. Donegal, and Staigue, Co. Kerry, hinting at some form of Celtic or Atlantic continuum of building traditions – a theme that has bubbled just below the surface of broch studies ever since.

The last major marker in nineteenth-century broch studies, and the one which signalled the end of the antiquarian period, was the publication in 1883 of *Scotland in Pagan Times: the Iron Age* by Joseph Anderson (Wilson's successor as Scotland's paramount prehistorian). In this immensely influential work, Anderson moved away from his former belief that brochs were Pictish structures of the fifth to ninth centuries AD, arguing instead that they could be dated to the period of Roman influence, in the first and second centuries AD. In making this change, Anderson was drawing on the lessons learned from the numerous, albeit often ramshackle, excavations of the preceding decades, and the many objects of Roman manufacture that they had produced.

Anderson's publication coincided with a lull in broch excavations as the Orcadian pioneers passed from the scene, and his work came to assume a rather reified status. Anderson saw brochs as great defensive towers, built over a short span of years to meet the security requirements of the local élite. This view was to stand essentially unchallenged for almost a century.

Brochs for the people

Following the death of George Petrie in 1875 active fieldwork in Orkney tailed off. Other areas had their own pioneers, generally those with land and time on their hands, such as Sir Francis Tress Barry in Caithness (who seems to have excavated at least 14 brochs; perhaps a record), Erskine Beveridge in North Uist (**6** & **7**) and the Countess de La Tour in Skye, but the initial excitement of discovery and debate, which is so clear in the mid-nineteenth century

6 *A summer visit to Dun Torcuill, a complex roundhouse in North Uist*

accounts, seems to have passed. Most fieldworkers seem to have accepted Anderson's assertions as to the date, origins and purpose of brochs with little question. There were, of course, some exceptions, including James Cursiter in Orkney who, as late as 1923, was setting out his alternative thesis that the brochs had been brought to Scotland by Phoenicians fleeing Atlantis before the last Ice Age. Cursiter's theories failed to attract much support.

It was not until the 1930s that the next major phase of fieldwork took off, much of it bound up with the emergence of 'public archaeology' and the desire to exhibit the remains of the more spectacular of these structures to a wider audience. For the first time state funds were made available to excavate and display these monuments, often in partnership with landowners and other benefactors. The excavations of the broch and its surrounding village at Midhowe on Rousay in Orkney, for example, were initially financed by a local landowner, Walter Grant, before the site was handed over to the state for conservation and display.

The complete excavation and consolidation of the highly complex broch of Gurness in Orkney (**colour plates 17** & **22**) was carried out over a period of ten years by a succession of excavators and involved input from the Society of Antiquaries of Scotland and funding from H.M. Office of Works. Explicit aims were to lay the site out for public view and to collect as large a body of artefacts as possible for display in the National Museum. As at Midhowe, the broch of Gurness was the centrepiece of a clustered village of smaller houses, all of which, along with the surrounding ramparts and ditches, were cleared of archaeological deposits and laid out for public gaze. The growing professionalisation of archaeology in Scotland, sadly, was not reflected in the excavation methods applied to this extraordinary site. Instead the highly sensitive deposits within the broch tower were emptied out by workmen in less than a month, with minimal recording of the stratified deposits inside.

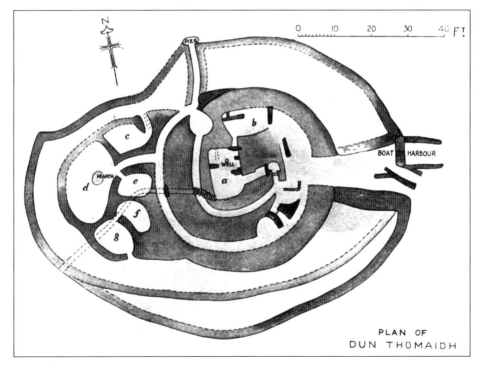

7 *Dun Thomaidh, North Uist. Erskine Beveridge's plan of the excavated remains at this islet-sited complex roundhouse indicates some of the difficulties that early excavators had in disentangling multi-period stone buildings. Presented as a single phase plan, the structures seem to make little sense. On the basis of comparisons with other sites in the Western Isles it is likely that the structures incorporate the accumulation of many centuries of building and rebuilding over the original roundhouse*

The 'Diffusionists'

While Joseph Anderson and his disciples had interpreted brochs as the indigenous products of native populations, subsequent generations of archaeologists had come increasingly to see major innovations in prehistory as the result of the movement or diffusion of ideas from outside. The main mechanisms by which such ideas were thought to have moved were invasion, migration and the colonisation of new territories by increasingly advanced societies. From a Scottish perspective, this meant the arrival of successive peoples from the south. Major cultural or technological innovations, for example the development of bronze-working, were thought generally to have had their origins in the Near East or around the fringes of the Mediterranean, and subsequently to have spread north and westwards to Europe's outer fringes.

The arguments over the diffusion of ideas, technologies and cultures versus their independent evolution or invention was nothing new. As early as the mid-nineteenth century, heavyweight European archaeologists like Jan Worsaae had been arguing for invasion as the prime mover of cultural change. Others, influenced by the evolutionary principles established by Darwin, contended that human populations everywhere had an innate tendency to evolve into increasingly complex and sophisticated societies. During the 1920s and 1930s, however, European archaeologists became increasingly preoccupied with the definition of prehistoric 'cultures', which could be identified with 'peoples' or ethnic groups, and with the mapping of their movement and spread. Whilst this way of looking at archaeological evidence has long since been superseded, it did at least provide the opportunity to view the archaeology of particular regions from a wider, European perspective.

Gordon Childe in his *Prehistory of Scotland*, first published in 1935, took a characteristically wide view of the broch question and set them, for the first time, in a wider north-west European context. Childe, who was then Abercromby Professor of Prehistoric Archaeology at Edinburgh University and arguably the most influential European archaeologist of his generation, recognised that brochs were just one element in a wider grouping of small stone forts which he termed the 'castle complex'. As well as encompassing the many less elaborate stone-walled duns and small enclosures of Atlantic Scotland, this terminology also tied the brochs to the wider distribution of small stone enclosures, notably the Cornish 'cliff-castles', stretching far down the western seaboard of Britain and beyond. Childe envisaged the brochs as the archaeological manifestation of a population movement into Atlantic Scotland from south-western Britain towards the end of the Iron Age. Even in his provocative experiment with an explicitly Marxist interpretation of Scottish prehistory, *Scotland before the Scots* published in 1946, where much stress was laid on internal social evolution, Childe still felt that the appearance of the brochs merited an invasionist explanation. This idea was based less on the brochs themselves, which plainly had no counterparts in the south, but rather on some of the small utilitarian objects found on excavations of broch sites. Confronted with a series of similarities in items such as weaving combs, triangular crucibles and bone dice, Childe felt that a 'real invasion of warlike chieftains with their retainers and their families is the most reasonable deduction'. So, rather than the defensive refuges of nervous natives envisaged by Anderson and others, Childe saw the brochs as the planted strongholds of an invading élite. Likening them to the mottes of medieval Norman invaders he saw their main purpose as being to 'overawe a subject population'.

Childe's work was hugely influential and set the tone for the next 40 years of research on the Atlantic Scottish Iron Age. Despite much lively debate over the precise homelands of the broch-builders, the motives behind their migration, and the detailed timetable of their arrival and spread, the next generation of Scottish prehistorians did not seriously question the basic premise that brochs were the products of southern incomers around the turn of the first millennium. Sir Lindsay Scott, writing in the 1940s, widened the field of possible colonisers to encompass the Breton tribes of north-west France, while his contemporary, T.C. Lethbridge, believed that eastern English peoples had played a role in the genesis of the 'broch culture'. Childe's successor as Abercromby Professor, Stuart Piggott, plumped for western France as the main point of origin, with north-west England as a stopping-off point for the emigrants en route to the Hebrides. Much depended on what one made of similarities in the pottery styles, bone tools and other items which made up the archaeological record in each area.

Despite this broad consensus over an intrusive origin for the brochs, there was some disagreement over their original form and function. Childe, like Anderson before him, had accepted the seemingly common sense view that, whether built by natives or incomers, these were unambiguously defensive structures. The first serious challenge to this orthodoxy came from Sir Lindsay Scott in his article *The Problem of the Brochs*, published in 1947. Scott argued that too much emphasis had been placed on the best-preserved, tower-like examples such as Mousa, of which he said 'there can be few structures which more grimly suggest a hold of desperate men'. Yet most brochs, Scott argued, survived as relatively low, squat ruins which displayed no evidence of ever having attained tower-like proportions. Indeed their locations, in pockets of relatively good farmland, and their limited defensibility, suggested to Scott that most brochs were primarily low-walled farmsteads rather than high-walled forts: towers like Mousa were a rather distracting minority. Scott's ideas marked a radical break with conventional wisdom and they were not well received by the archaeological establishment. However, despite his lack of impact at the time, Scott's ideas foreshadowed much of what was to come in the modern phase of broch research.

From the 1960s the diffusionist viewpoint was championed by Euan MacKie, who dominated the field through a range of excavations and interpretative papers. In MacKie's version of the diffusionist model, the broch culture was the product of influence from southern England (specifically Wessex), and north-west France (specifically the *Veneti* of Brittany). In MacKie's view, these southern migrants introduced a range of cultural innovations during the first century BC and were prime movers in the development of the broch tower from the more modest drystone buildings that were already being built by the indigenous population of Atlantic Scotland.

As well as being concerned with the cultural origins of the broch-builders, MacKie's work also focused on the details of their architectural development within Atlantic Scotland. Arguing on the basis of what he regarded as successive advances in their design and structural stability (most importantly the replacement of early ground-galleried brochs by brochs with solid wall bases), MacKie suggested that the earliest brochs were to be found in the Hebrides, whence they spread northwards to Orkney and Shetland. This view was in contrast to the more generally held belief that brochs had probably originated in the north mainland or Northern Isles, where they are found in the greatest densities.

The appliance of science

Although the diffusionist principles underlying the interpretation of brochs changed little from the 1930s to the 1970s, a great deal of progress was made over that period in terms of data collection and analysis. Field surveys carried out by the Royal Commission on the Ancient and Historical Monuments of Scotland (RCAHMS) made a wealth of data available for study. Particularly important was their authoritative inventory of the field monuments of Orkney and Shetland, published in 1946. Shortly thereafter Angus Graham published *Some observations on the brochs* in which he drew together all the available facts and figures relating to the structure and variation of brochs across the whole of Atlantic Scotland. His work forms the basis for much of the discussion in chapter 3. The greatest advances, however, were to come through the first scientific excavations of broch sites, particularly the work of John Hamilton of the Ministry of Works, at the sites of Jarlshof and Clickhimin in Shetland (**colour plates 1 & 23**).

Although a pioneer in the application of scientific techniques to broch excavation, Hamilton remained firmly within the diffusionist school of interpretation. He saw brochs as essentially military structures which had evolved from larger drystone forts with their ultimate origins in the Alpine area around 800-500 BC (**8**). From there they spread, via southern France and Iberia, along the Atlantic sea routes to Ireland and, ultimately, Atlantic Scotland. Hamilton believed that the broch tower itself was developed locally,

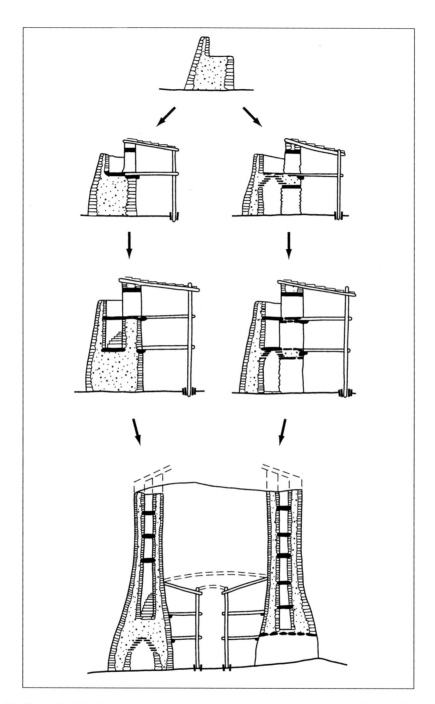

8 *Hamilton believed that broch towers were in essence forts and that their architecture had evolved from earlier simpler rampart forms which could be traced back through Iberia and southern France ultimately to central Europe. This simplified version of one his drawings shows how he saw the development from a simple stone-faced rampart, through ramparts with timber lean-to buildings, to the eventual broch tower with its (conjectural) timber lean-to constructions. This is a typical scheme of the diffusionist period of broch studies, but would have few adherents today*

probably in Orkney, from a background of experimentation with various forms of defensive architecture.

Hamilton's excavations at Jarlshof, from 1949-52, were on a site already much disturbed by antiquarian digging, and the deposits inside the broch tower itself had been more or less completely destroyed. Nonetheless, Hamilton's work on adjacent areas of the site revealed a complex stratigraphic sequence whereby a broch tower was replaced by a succession of later structures of broadly wheelhouse form (see chapter 7). The latest Iron Age buildings were themselves replaced by a Viking farmstead in the ninth century AD. Hamilton's report summarised the results both of his own work and that of earlier excavators, and provided a benchmark in the development of broch studies. Although Jarlshof had rich evidence for Bronze Age activity, however, the immediately pre-broch deposits were sterile sand, suggesting a break in occupation. To explore the antecedents of the brochs, Hamilton had to look elsewhere.

The year after completing his work at Jarlshof, Hamilton began work on the islet-sited broch tower of Clickhimin on the outskirts of Lerwick. Like Jarlshof, the site had been tinkered with in the past, firstly by members of the Shetland Literary Society in 1861 and secondly by the Ministry of Works in the early 1900s, but overall these early investigations had done less damage than

9 *Alan Sorrell's reconstruction drawing of Clickhimin, Shetland, is based on Hamilton's interpretation of the buildings. It shows the broch tower with a partial roof, set within a heavily enclosed islet and fronted by the blockhouse*

might have been expected. Hamilton's work again revealed an apparently lengthy and complex history of occupation. To begin with, a small oval house, similar to the Late Bronze Age buildings at Jarlshof, seems to have occupied the site. This may have been replaced by a stone roundhouse during the Early Iron Age, though the evidence is equivocal. The subsequent phases, however, are both more significant and more controversial. Hamilton believed that new arrivals from the south took over the site and built the great stone rampart which now surrounds it. During the Iron Age, in Hamilton's view, this rampart would have sheltered a series of internal timber ranges. Inside the entrance to this fortified enclosure was built an impressive stone 'blockhouse' (**colour plate 6**). This massive structure seemed to pre-figure the architecture of brochs in having both a scarcement ledge and intramural cells. Hamilton believed that, like the enclosing wall, the blockhouse would have had a timber lean-to construction to its rear. Some time later, the broch tower itself was constructed behind the blockhouse. In Hamilton's view this represented the arrival of yet another set of new people (**9**).

Hamilton's view of the sequence at Clickhimin has been challenged by later commentators, who have suggested that the sequence of events may have been rather simpler than first suggested. Even from Hamilton's published records, for example, it is possible to argue that the blockhouse may in fact have been built at the same time as the broch tower, or even slightly later. Indeed, the whole conception of broch tower, blockhouse, enclosing wall and timber ranges may have been implanted as one major building operation.

These uncertainties would tend now to weaken the argument for the role of blockhouses, like that at Clickhimin, as ancestral to broch towers. At the time, however, Hamilton's work seemed to suggest that the evidence for the evolution of the broch tower was to be found in the Northern Isles (even if its inspiration was still generally thought to be foreign). This view was shortly to be challenged, however, by the work of Euan MacKie whose fieldwork began in the early 1960s, only a few years after Hamilton's own excavations in Shetland had ceased.

MacKie sought to demonstrate an alternative sequence of development focusing on the west coast. Through a combination of site examination and selective excavation, MacKie developed the belief that the ground-galleried brochs found most commonly in the Hebrides had developed from a still earlier type of structure known as the 'semi-broch'. These C- or D-shaped structures are found exclusively on cliff edges or other precipitous slopes, suggesting to many observers that they were in fact more or less normal round-houses of which one half had simply fallen away (**10**). Mackie, however, believed that these were in fact a genuine class of building ancestral to brochs.

In an attempt to prove his ideas, MacKie excavated two of these 'semi-brochs': Dun Ardtreck in Skye and Dun an Ruigh Ruaidh, Loch Broom. From these he was able to obtain a number of radiocarbon dates which

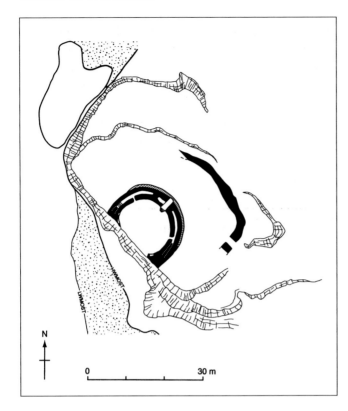

10 *This simplified plan shows the 'semi-broch' of Dun Ardtreck in Skye. Many archaeologists would interpret such structures as former roundhouses which have been eroded by the sea. According to the 'semi-broch' theory, however, they represent a genuine class of open-sided, C- or D-shaped buildings set on exposed cliff edges. If so, their inhabitants would have been chilly indeed*

suggested to him that these structures were earlier than the mid-first century BC (and thus, in his view, earlier than the brochs). The semi-broch theory, however, has not been well-received. Many archaeologists remain unconvinced that MacKie's semi-brochs are anything other than partially eroded round-houses, and the radiocarbon dates from MacKie's excavations are open to a wide range of possible interpretations.

More influential was MacKie's work at Dun Mor Vaul on Tiree, in the early 1960s. This first scientific excavation of a western broch was explicitly designed to establish a Hebridean sequence comparable with that achieved by Hamilton in Shetland. It revealed a wealth of evidence both for the development of the building and the material culture of the inhabitants, even though the site lacked the size and structural complexity of Jarlshof and Clickhimin. Collectively, Hamilton and MacKie's excavations were to provide the baseline for much modern study of these structures.

Radiocarbon and the long chronology

During the 1960s, even as MacKie was developing his detailed model for the genesis of the brochs, the general diffusionist approach to archaeological interpretation was coming under attack. Increasingly archaeologists had come to recognise that human societies operated in a rather more complex way than earlier generations had often allowed, and that subtler models had to be constructed to explain the nature of change in prehistoric societies. In particular, the notion that change was invariably the product of migration and invasion had collapsed to the point that these concepts became almost taboo for a whole generation of archaeologists. Instead trade, exchange and various forms of social interaction became the more commonly favoured explanations for the spread of ideas in prehistory. Local innovation and the dynamic nature of prehistoric societies came increasingly to the fore, particularly as radiocarbon dating began to show that many ideas thought to have diffused from the classical world or the Near East were in fact entirely home-grown. For example, the megalithic tombs of north-west Europe were shown to pre-date the pyramids of Egypt of which they were previously thought to have been a pale reflection. Similarly it became clear that the earliest copper metallurgy was invented in Europe, independent from Near East or Mediterranean influence.

The backlash against diffusionism, however, was slow to reach the by now rather specialised world of broch studies. It was not until the early 1970s that a series of papers by David Clarke began systematically to demonstrate the weaknesses of the diffusionist accounts of the origins of brochs. Superficial similarities between objects such as bone dice and certain pottery vessels from both Wessex and Atlantic Scotland were shown to be either unconvincing when examined in detail, or else so general as to be largely meaningless. Yet it was not until the late 1970s that the diffusionist framework was finally to collapse. As elsewhere, it was radiocarbon dating that was to provide the killer blow.

Although radiocarbon dating had been developed in the United States during the late 1940s, its application in British archaeology only really took off during the 1960s. Euan MacKie himself was one of the first to apply the new technique to the problems of Scottish prehistory, obtaining several radiocarbon dates from his excavations at various sites on the west coast and Inner Hebrides in the late 1960s and '70s. Interpretation of these early dates was beset with difficulties, however, and the margins of error were generally too wide to be of much use.

The real impact of radiocarbon dating came with a new wave of excavations carried out principally by John Hedges and his collaborators in Orkney. In an impressive burst of work in the late 1970s, Hedges and his collaborators were to completely excavate two previously unknown 'broch' sites: firstly Bu, an isolated roundhouse, and secondly the complex multi-phase broch village of Howe. They also completed the publication of the 1930s excavations at Gurness and conducted a major re-evaluation of the brochs of Orkney in general. For all the new information and insights generated by this work, however, one overwhelming fact stood out. The radiocarbon dates proved that Bu was not built by incomers from the south during the first century BC. In fact, it was built many centuries earlier, some time between 800–400 BC. With the dating of Bu it became clear that, rather than being a short-lived product of an intrusive population, broch towers had developed locally over more than half a millennium. With this realisation the study of the Atlantic Scottish Iron Age entered its present phase. The chapters which follow set out the new picture which has since begun to emerge.

2

FROM ROUNDHOUSE
TO TOWER

For much of the twentieth century archaeologists saw the broch towers as an alien imposition on the Scottish landscape, the products of aristocratic warrior invaders from the far south. With the burst of excavation in Orkney in the late 1970s, however, and the discovery that structures ancestral to broch towers could be dated as early as 600 BC, it became apparent that these invasionist ideas were no longer adequate. Over the past 20 years, further excavation and survey in various parts of northern and western Scotland has begun to fill out a new picture, one of local innovation and structural evolution.

The roundhouse tradition

Perhaps the most striking feature of the Bronze Age and Iron Age landscapes of Scotland is the sheer number and variety of roundhouses. While the broch towers and other Atlantic roundhouses of the north and west may be the best known, they were by no means the earliest or most numerous. During the Iron Age, Atlantic roundhouses were simply the northernmost manifestation of a much wider architectural tradition.

When seen from a European perspective, circular houses appear as a distinctively British phenomenon. While many hundreds of Bronze and Iron Age farmsteads, hamlets and villages have been identified along the facing coasts of continental Europe, these are overwhelmingly dominated by large rectangular timber buildings. By contrast, from around 1800 BC, communities throughout Britain were building roundhouses. Over time this roundhouse architectural tradition was to give rise to a diverse range of forms, varying from region to region (**11** & **12**). Indeed, roundhouse architecture was to remain the characteristic settlement form in Britain for around 2,000 years, until new cultural influences ushered in a range of predominantly rectangular structural forms during the Roman period.

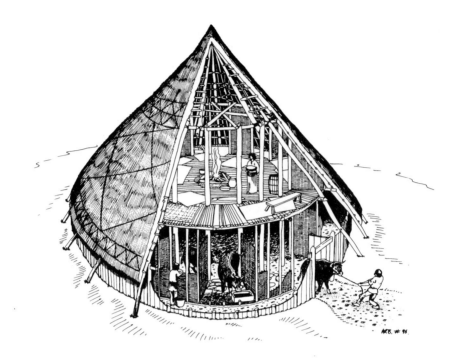

11 *This cut-away drawing gives some idea of the size and scale of the timber roundhouses of southern Scotland. This one is reconstructed as a two storey 'byre-house'*

12 *Many timber roundhouses in the south-west and central Highlands of Scotland occupied artificial islets known as crannogs. The development of these structures runs in parallel to the Atlantic roundhouses of the north and west*

Within Scotland we can identify a range of roundhouse building styles. Broch towers form part of the wider Atlantic roundhouse tradition, characterised by massively-built stone walls. In south and east Scotland, timber roundhouses are more common, and a whole range of variants can be identified in different regions and in different periods. Throughout the uplands, roundhouses with low, stone-faced earthen walls are common, often forming loosely aggregated settlements. These 'hut circles' overlap in their distribution with Atlantic roundhouses, but are fairly distinct in terms of their less massive construction and the earthen make-up of their walls.

Whereas ruinous Atlantic roundhouses proved difficult for later farmers to shift, the predominantly timber roundhouses in the south and east presented no such problems. Once the superstructure had decayed or been dismantled, the sites of these former roundhouses could be ploughed over and flattened, removing all surface traces (**13**). For the archaeologist, the best that can usually

13 *Timber roundhouses that might once have been as prominent in their lowland landscapes as Atlantic roundhouses were in the north and west have been all but obliterated from the modern landscape. Traces of most timber roundhouses survive only under the plough-soil where, under certain weather and crop conditions, they might be recognised as crop marks from aerial photography*

be hoped for are the remains of post-holes and occasionally sunken floors preserved below the modern plough-soil. Yet originally these timber buildings could equal or exceed the diameter (and thus the floor area) of many Atlantic roundhouses (**14**). Indeed, some of the larger roundhouses of around 16m in diameter would have contained twice as much floor space as the ground floor of the average modern semi-detached house.

The three-dimensional scale of these buildings can only really be appreciated by visiting full-scale reconstructions, as at Butser Farm in Hampshire or the Archaeolink Prehistory Park in Aberdeenshire. Indeed, experimental reconstruction of Iron Age roundhouses has revolutionised our understanding of these buildings. Despite variations in size and building style, prehistoric roundhouses share some fundamental structural principles which form the basis for any reconstruction. The roofing, for example, is largely dictated by the basic roundhouse form; essentially the buildings comprise a cone (the roof) placed upon a cylinder (the walls). Support for the roof may come from

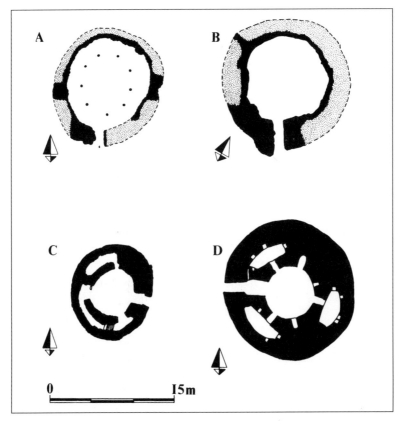

14 *These comparative plans show two hut circles from Kilphedir in Sutherland (a and b) at the same scale as the complex roundhouse of Dun Bharabhat (c) and the broch tower of Mousa (d). In these particular cases the hut circles enclose significantly greater internal areas*

the outer walls (which may be of timber, earth or stone), or from an inner ring of posts. The sole break in the basic geometry of the house is the entrance, of which there is usually only one, sometimes with a protruding porch. From the diameters and depths of the excavated post-holes it is often possible to calculate the size of the original timbers and in some cases the likely height to which they would have stood above the floor. In exceptional cases the remains of charred posts may show which species of tree was used in construction.

Generally the main weight of the roof was taken by an inner ring of stout posts, while a wall of wattle and daub supported by slighter posts provided weather-proofing. In upland areas the wall was often built of earth or stone, providing extra insulation and also saving on timber. The diameters of the oak posts used for the inner ring of an excavated roundhouse at Pimperne Down, in the chalklands of Wessex, suggest that they were obtained from trees around 40 years old. Even older trees would have been required for the massive porch posts. The outer walls, by contrast, were built of long, straight stakes, most likely the thinnings from carefully managed woodland.

Experiment has also shown subtler details. For example, it is unlikely that these buildings had any need for a smoke-hole in the roof. Aside from letting in the rain, such a gap would tend to create an updraft carrying sparks from the central fire dangerously upwards into the thatch. Instead, it appears that smoke would have been allowed to drift slowly upwards, filling the upper parts of the building, gradually percolating through the thatch (and, as a useful by-product, keeping it free of vermin). It is perhaps not fanciful to imagine that food could have been preserved by smoking and drying in these upper reaches of the house.

Full-scale reconstructions have also demonstrated the durability of such buildings. For example, a timber roundhouse reconstructed at Butser Farm, based on the excavated example from Pimperne, survived the 1987 hurricane with few ill effects. With proper care and maintenance these roundhouses would probably have stood for many generations. Indeed Peter Reynolds, Director of the Butser Project, estimated that some may have been occupied for as much as a century. All in all then, these timber roundhouses could be substantial, long-lived, wind- and water-tight buildings.

The Bronze Age roundhouses of northern Scotland

Hut circles with walls of stone and earth have long been recognised as a feature of the upland landscapes of northern and eastern Scotland, where the lack of later intensive agriculture has allowed many to survive as visible features in the landscape (**15**). Ordnance Survey maps abound with depictions of these hut circles and associated field systems, and around 2,000 or more are known in

15 *This snow-covered scene close to Pitcarmick in Perthshire contains an extensive landscape of hut circles, clearance cairns and field walls. These are remnants of a Bronze Age push into the uplands of Scotland which saw the farming of many areas that would be considered highly marginal today. Indeed it is the lack of intensive land use in the medieval and modern periods which has led to the survival of these remains*

Sutherland alone. Yet it is only fairly recently that their significance has begun to be fully realised through detailed survey and modern excavation.

Excavations during the 1980s at Achany Glen, near Lairg in Sutherland, revealed a series of roundhouses mostly dating to between 2000-1000 BC. The form of these buildings varied from simple wigwam-like constructions, where the rafters of the roof rested directly on the ground surface, to more substantial roundhouses with walls of earth and stone. The floors often seem to have been organised in radial fashion, with small rooms or bays leading off from a central area where the main hearth burned. In terms of floor area, the houses at Achany Glen are well within the range of the later Atlantic roundhouses and, even though their walls were much less massively-built, the rather disparaging term 'hut circle' does not do them justice. Judging by their overall diameters and assuming that they were roofed at a 45-degree pitch, some of these Bronze Age roundhouses would have had roofs standing around 7m tall at their apex and would have been extremely impressive within their local landscapes.

Later Bronze Age houses in the Northern and Western Isles

Although Bronze Age hut circles are densely distributed in the uplands of mainland Scotland, and along the west coast, they are less common in the Northern Isles where the greatest numbers of Atlantic roundhouses are subsequently to be found. Indeed, the houses of the Bronze Age inhabitants of Orkney and Shetland seem to have been quite different, preserving local traditions of building and domestic organisation that can be traced back to the Neolithic period. The Late Bronze Age houses excavated at Jarlshof in Shetland, for example, were small and cellular in layout with thick stone walls (**16**). Houses like this are found widely across Shetland, often as isolated farmsteads, but sometimes in small clusters.

Although generally regarded as a Bronze Age tradition, this form of structure appears to survive well into the Iron Age contemporary with Atlantic roundhouses. Although long suspected, this survival has recently been proved by excavations at the non-broch settlement of Kebister in Shetland, where houses in the cellular tradition represent the main living quarters right through the Iron Age. The extent of this sort of survival is far from clear, perhaps because so much attention has been focused on the excavation of the more obvious Atlantic roundhouse settlements, but it may very well be that these houses develop seamlessly into the distinctive cellular houses found on the Iron Age broch villages like Gurness (chapter 5). Although Bronze Age cellular houses are best known in the Northern Isles, and especially in Shetland, similar structures have been found elsewhere in Atlantic Scotland, for example at Ceann nan Clachan in North Uist, and Cladh Hallan in South Uist, where they seemingly date to the latest part of the Bronze Age.

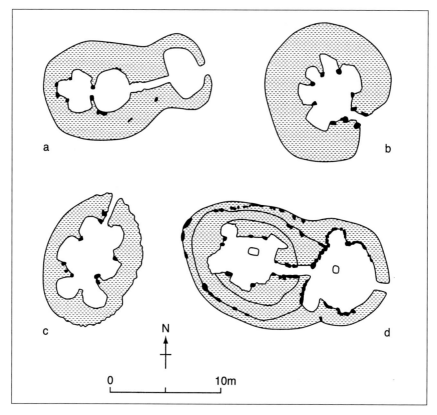

16 *Late Bronze Age houses in the Northern Isles were generally cellular structures. The following are all from Shetland: a. Yoxie, b. Sulma Water, c. Gravlaba, d. the 'Benie Hoose'*

From a purely functional point of view we can point to three main concerns apparent in the design of these Bronze Age buildings. The first is a concern with insulation, reflected in the thick stone walls, which were often increased in thickness during the lifetime of the building. The second is the need to conserve timber which would presumably have been a scarce resource in the Northern Isles even in the Bronze Age. Generally the interiors of the Bronze Age houses are small and cellular, meaning that individual cells can be roofed by stone corbelling and that short lengths of timber are all that is needed to roof the main central living spaces. Local supplies of driftwood would usually have been sufficient to provide the modest timbers required for roofing. Thirdly, the walls and roofs of these buildings would have been fairly low to the ground, perhaps to prevent too much exposure to the high winds commonly experienced in the region.

There could of course be other, less functionally determined reasons for the form of these Bronze Age houses. For example, the cellular interiors may reflect a desire to break up the domestic space in order to segregate different activities or different groups of people. The thick walls may have been intended to create an impression of bulk, to make the buildings seem more imposing to the visitor. Most probably there was considerable interplay between these social and functional factors over the course of the Bronze Age resulting in a range of variations on the main architectural theme of low-walled, oval buildings with cellular interiors. What is clear is that by the early centuries of the first millennium BC, the communities of the Northern Isles had a long-established architectural tradition well-tailored to the demands of their North Atlantic environment. It is this apparently stable and well-adapted architectural background that makes the adoption of the roundhouse during the Early Iron Age so remarkable.

Bu and the first Atlantic roundhouses

The rescue excavations at Bu in Orkney, carried out by John Hedges and his team over a few weeks in 1978, were to revolutionise the study of the Atlantic Scottish Iron Age. The proposed removal of a prominent stony mound in a farmer's field had prompted what appeared to be a fairly routine salvage exercise. Once work began, however, it quickly became clear that the mound contained a massive roundhouse which, at the time of excavation, was thought to be a broch. It was only later, when the radiocarbon dates had been processed, that the true significance of the site became clear. The radiocarbon dates demonstrated beyond reasonable doubt that the structure had been built, occupied and abandoned during the period 800–400 BC.

The walls of the Bu roundhouse show little sign of ever having been tall or tower-like. They lack any of the complex features commonly associated with broch architecture. For example, there were no intra-mural cells, galleries or stairs, and no sign of a scarcement ledge. Indeed it was only the overall size, shape and immense thickness of the drystone walls that led the excavators initially to believe that they had found a broch. At the time of excavation it was assumed that this lack of complexity was no more than the result of poor preservation. The walls survived only to around 1.5m high, and any former galleries or stairs could simply have been lost through collapse and stone-robbing. There were other indications, however, that Bu had never been a particularly tall building. Most importantly, the salvage nature of the excavation and the prospect of the imminent demolition of the structure, allowed the excavators to dismantle sections of the walling under controlled conditions. This exercise, which had never before been attempted on previous broch excavations, revealed that rather than being built as one operation, the 5m-wide wall was a composite construction. An inner core of walling, some 3m thick, with its own inner and outer faces, had been refaced both internally and externally to produce a progressively thicker wall. The original core of walling would clearly not have supported a tower-like superstructure, so it seems that Bu was probably designed as a roundhouse of quite modest height. The available rubble on the site might have been enough to have made the walls up to around 2m high, and stone-robbing may well have removed some more, but all in all we probably have to assume that the original building was single storey and relatively low-walled.

The realisation that Bu was an Early Iron Age roundhouse of modest height has enormous implications for wider interpretations of the Atlantic Scottish Iron Age. The vast majority of structures recorded as brochs have no more indications of architectural complexity than were present at Bu. Whereas in the past these were generally thought to have been poorly preserved broch towers, we now have to allow that an unknowable proportion of them may have been much simpler, low-walled roundhouses, potentially of quite early date.

The excavations at Bu provide us with a remarkably clear picture of an early roundhouse settlement in Orkney. This is mainly due to the extremely high level of survival of the internal fixtures and fittings which had been built using local Orkney flagstones. The internal space at Bu was more or less circular, measuring around 10m by 9m, with an internal area of around 70m² which puts it in the same general range as the Bronze Age roundhouses of Sutherland. The most striking feature of the interior was the way that the internal space was fragmented (**17**). Rather than experiencing a large open circular space, the visitor to Bu would have been constantly enclosed within a network of numerous small rooms or compartments. These were divided by screens of flagstones set on edge and bedded into foundation trenches wedged with smaller chocking stones. Most of these flagstone partitions had been either removed or broken up by later generations in search of good building stone, so it is impossible to be sure how high they would have been. Judging from other Orcadian sites where flagstone partitions are used (for example, Midhowe, see chapter 5) they may well have been up to 1.8m tall, that is around head height for an adult, and may have helped support the timber roofing structure of the roundhouse.

The floor plan at Bu is probably best explained by describing the experience of a visitor to the roundhouse. On first entering, the visitor would pass along the narrow entrance (**17**), encountering a timber door set halfway down the entrance passage. What seems to have been a blocked entrance in this passage may signify the former presence of a small 'guard' cell on the visitor's right, but this could not be confirmed by excavation. Once through the entrance passage, the visitor would have entered a small paved 'vestibule' from which led several doors. To the left was a doorway leading directly into the heart of the building: a large, more or less circular room which contained an enormous hearth, a cooking tank and slab-built cupboard. The floors here were all of bare earth, probably covered over with straw or matting when the building was occupied. This seems to have been the part of the house in which

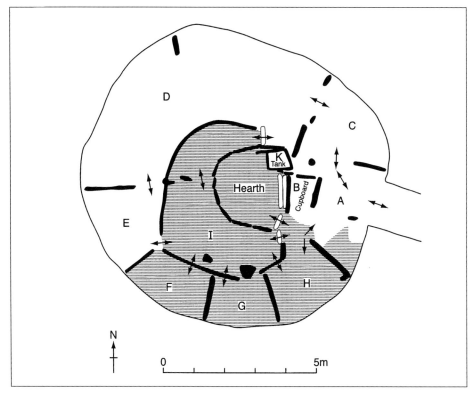

17 *This simplified drawing of the floor plan of Bu roundhouse is based on an original version by the excavator but interprets the use of the building slightly differently. The unshaded areas are paved. It appears that the central area was the main living space, while a series of 'box-beds' opened onto it from the south. The long, paved room to the north may have been a byre*

the inhabitants would have spent much of their time, preparing food, cooking, eating and talking, and warming themselves by the fire. Leading off from this central area were three small cubicles fronted by stone slabs. These may very well have been sleeping areas, the slabs serving to retain a comfortable depth of soft bedding material.

If, instead of turning left into the warm central area, the visitor turned to the right, they would have passed through a second doorway into a small paved room which in turn gave access to a longer, paved chamber running around the arc of the roundhouse wall. The excavations gave little clue as to the function of these peripheral spaces, but one strong possibility is that they were designed not for human habitation but for animals. Bones of cattle, sheep and pigs were all found at Bu, showing that the inhabitants had a strong pastoral element to their economy. It is possible that some of these animals were stalled within the house, perhaps over the winter or at other specific times of year, where they, like their keepers, could be protected from the elements. This sort of arrangement could explain the stone paving in these areas, which would have allowed mucking out, and the presence of drains revealed below the one small area of paving which the excavators were able to remove. As we shall see in chapter 3, this 'byre-house' design was to be a recurrent theme in the development of Atlantic roundhouse architecture.

Although there are few reliable floor-plans from the early excavations of broch sites in Orkney, there are some indications that the layout at Bu may not be unique. The site of Burrian Russland on Harray, for example, was cleared out by James Farrer in 1866 and the only useful records are drawings by his contemporary, George Petrie. Petrie's plan and sketch show a central area with hearth and tank, flanked to the north by a long curving room just as at Bu (although the two rooms are separated by a built wall rather than the flagstone partitions seen at Bu). Also mirroring the situation at Bu are three smaller cubicles leading off to the south of the central area which may have been for sleeping. The situation is almost exactly repeated at the site of Burroughston on Shapinsay, also emptied in the 1860s and recorded by Petrie. Overall the correspondence between these three sites is striking, although the lack of further detailed information on what was found at Burrian and Burroughston is frustrating. As well as suggesting that the spatial organisation of Orcadian roundhouses may have adhered to well-established social norms, these similarities may also imply that Burroughston and Burrian, like Bu, are rather earlier in date than was previously assumed.

The roundhouse revolution

The application of radiocarbon dating to excavated sites in Scotland has become routine in recent years and early dates have now been obtained for a range of other roundhouses. A poorly preserved roundhouse at Pierowall in Orkney, for example, has been shown to date to broadly the same period as Bu, as has a roundhouse excavated in the eroding coastal edge at the site of St Boniface Church. Simple, thick-walled Atlantic roundhouses seem, therefore, to have been built in some numbers in Orkney during the early part of the Iron Age.

Several other early roundhouses seem to have had rather less massive walls. One such structure had been built into the ruins of a Neolithic chambered tomb at Quanterness, while a few others can be tentatively identified in the older literature. There are not yet enough high quality modern excavations to enable us to disentangle the detail of this early period of roundhouse-building. It is tempting to suggest that the thin-walled roundhouses may have been adopted first with the thicker-walled examples being developed slightly later. Although this cannot be demonstrated with any great confidence, the progressive thickening of the roundhouse walls at Bu may hint that such a development occurred. Alternatively, different communities may simply have built roundhouses of varying dimensions and complexity in accordance with their needs and capabilities. Whatever the detail of the process, however, the concept of the roundhouse had arrived.

These early roundhouses shared a number of characteristics. Firstly, they appear to have been isolated, unenclosed farmsteads. Secondly, they appear to have been structurally simple, lacking most of the diagnostic traits of broch architecture. Presumably they were relatively low buildings similar in outward appearance to the broadly contemporary thick-walled hut circles of Sutherland.

In several ways the design and construction of the first Atlantic roundhouses marks a complete break with earlier architectural forms in the Northern Isles. Whereas the Bronze Age structures tended to be cellular in construction, with short roofing spans requiring few long timbers, the roundhouse builders made no such allowances – substantial timbers would have been required to roof the 10m span of the roundhouse at Bu. Whereas the Bronze Age houses were low-walled or even partly set into the ground, minimising exposure to the elements, the first Atlantic roundhouses stood to heights of 2m or more, with roofs rising perhaps 5m or more higher still. Although their massively thick walls would have provided some degree of insulation, these structures were clearly not built with heat conservation or economy of resources in mind.

Despite these very marked structural differences, however, the internal organisation of the early roundhouses had much in common with earlier buildings. As we have seen, the interior at Bu was sub-divided into a complex pattern of small rooms and cells that bore little obvious relation to the circularity of the roundhouse itself. Instead it seems as if the traditional cellular arrangement, with fragmented spaces and discrete activity areas, had been squeezed into the interior of the new roundhouse. The major distinction between the first Atlantic roundhouses and the Bronze Age cellular structures seems, therefore, to have been in the outward appearance of the buildings and the resources required for their construction. Life inside the house may have carried on according to much the same conventions as it had before. This rather suggests that it was the indigenous population of Orkney who had adopted the roundhouse form of building from their mainland neighbours.

Assuming that there was no significant change in population, the impetus for the change was presumably based on factors internal to the Later Bronze Age societies of Orkney. Given that the main impact of the roundhouse form lay in its potential to create monumental, impressive and (at least initially) exotic buildings, it may be that its adoption reflected an increased level of competition between Orcadian communities. Building highly visible, prominent structures which manifestly flouted environmental conditions and consumed large quantities of scarce resources may have been one way in which certain groups tried to impose their presence on the landscape and mark themselves out as particularly important, powerful or wealthy. The early roundhouses, however, were clearly not defensive in intent, as they were not particularly high-walled and had no external defences. Rather than signalling military conflict between hostile groups, this suggests that Atlantic roundhouses reflected the pretensions of neighbouring farmers, each trying to achieve social pre-eminence and perhaps hoping to bolster their claims to land and resources.

Crosskirk and the beginnings of complexity

The first Atlantic roundhouses represented a break from the long-established Bronze Age building traditions of the Northern Isles. Domestic architecture now had the potential to be monumental in scale and provided the opportunity for the display of status and prestige. The trend towards increasing monumentality that we see, for example, in the progressive thickening of the roundhouse walls at Bu, was to continue over the next few centuries with the appearance of complex Atlantic roundhouses in which the distinctive features we associate with broch architecture made their first appearance.

From around 500-200 BC, complex roundhouses began to be built in various parts of Atlantic Scotland. One of the best known is the coastal site of Crosskirk in Caithness which was excavated by Horace Fairhurst of Glasgow University between 1966 and 1972. When work began, it was believed that Crosskirk was a ruined broch tower in the traditional mould but, as excavation progressed, it became apparent that this structure could never have been any sort of tower. Although its walls were nearly 6m thick in places they had a core of clay, earth, rubble and even domestic refuse, which could never have supported a massive stone superstructure. Indeed, the apparent thickness of the wall was also rather misleading since, as at Bu, the original wall had been progressively thickened by the addition of outer casings of stonework. Although these have often been viewed as attempts to buttress and support walls which (in the case of Crosskirk at least) were rather poorly built and manifestly unstable, it is hard to see how they would have functioned in this way. These casings are generally no more than skins of walling butting the original roundhouse wall. Without being bonded into the original structure, they would have provided virtually no protection against subsidence or collapse – at best they would have sheltered the original walls from weathering and perhaps provided a little extra insulation. Overall, however, it seems most likely that they were simply intended to make the structure seem bigger and thus more impressive to the visitor.

Taking all the available evidence into account, Fairhurst suggested that the Crosskirk roundhouse would not have been stable above around 4.5m in height. This may have been just about tall enough to accommodate some form of upper floor, but it was still less than half the height of classic broch towers such as Mousa. Indeed, in terms of its external appearance, Crosskirk would have looked much like Bu and the other early Orcadian roundhouses. Nonetheless, unlike Bu, the Crosskirk roundhouse contained a number of features commonly associated with broch architecture (**18**). The entrance passage, for example, contained an opening to a small guard cell, and a second intra-mural cell could be accessed from inside the roundhouse. A series of steps formed part of an intra-mural staircase which may have given access to the wall-head or some form of upper floor. More unusually, a stone ladder recessed into the north wall opposite the entrance to the intra-mural stair seems to have provided additional access either to the wall-head or an upper floor.

Crosskirk also differed from the early Orcadian roundhouses in that it did not stand alone. From the start the roundhouse, where not protected by the cliff edge, was fronted by a large stone-faced rampart and ditch and the intervening space may have accommodated out-buildings of some form. The outworks were clearly not intended to be seriously defensive as they decreased in size away from the entrance until they became little more than a line of slabs. The aim seems to have been to impress visitors who might pass through the main gateway rather than to deter intruders.

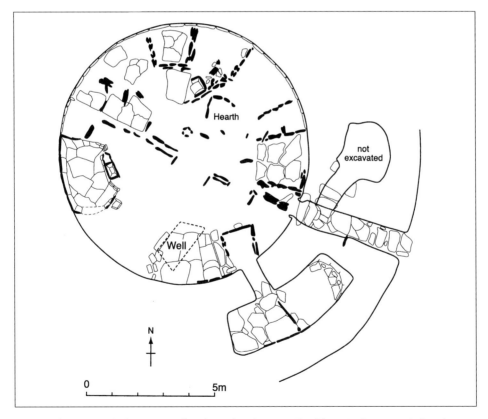

18 *The floor at Crosskirk is not as well understood as the one at Bu. The main features are indicated on this simplified plan, but they may not all have been in use at the same time*

As with Bu, one of the most surprising aspects of the work at Crosskirk was its sequence of radiocarbon dates which are remarkably early (although frustratingly imprecise). One in particular, from the primary floor of the roundhouse, seems to indicate occupation between around 760-260 BC. At the time Fairhurst dismissed this date as being improbably early, since the prevailing view was that brochs had been introduced by invaders during the first century BC. The date in question was actually obtained from compressed plant material under a large flagstone which apparently formed part of the earliest roundhouse floor. Although Fairhurst subsequently suggested that this feature may have been a relic from a pre-roundhouse occupation on the site, this was simply because the date seemed too early for the prevailing ideas on the origins of brochs. In the light of more recent work at Bu and elsewhere, it now seems perfectly possible that the date may be valid after all.

Other dates from the site provide some limited support for this view. For example, there are two radiocarbon dates from a late phase of one of the outbuildings which suggest that it was occupied in the last couple of centuries BC. This may not seem terribly significant until it is realised that this outbuilding overlies an earlier one, which overlies a still earlier one, which overlies an outer casing applied to the roundhouse wall some unknown time after its construction. In other words, a good deal had happened on the site between the building of the roundhouse and the activity to which these radiocarbon dates relate. Other radiocarbon dates from Crosskirk show that its occupation certainly continued into the early centuries AD, and this is backed up by a small assemblage of Roman pottery from the later phases of occupation.

The interior area at Crosskirk was some 10m or so in diameter, more or less the same as at Bu, but the much longer period of occupation meant that the primary floor was greatly disturbed, and it is virtually impossible to establish which of the early features are absolutely contemporary. Over time, the interior was persistently remodelled and the earlier floors periodically churned up, creating some major problems of interpretation for the excavator. Fairhurst's own reconstruction of the primary plan combines features which, if in use at the same time, would have nearly blocked the entrance to the roundhouse, so it has to be treated with some caution (**18**). Nonetheless, it is fairly clear that the building had a more or less binary plan, bisected by a line of upright flagstones. In the northern half, there was a substantial hearth and a series of radial rooms or compartments, with a mix of earth and flagstone floors. This seems to have been the main domestic area where the inhabitants would have cooked, eaten and slept. The southern half was also sub-divided and had, in one area, a sunken paved floor which may have been used for threshing grain. It is possible that animals may have been kept in this part of the building as well, but the evidence is really too slight to draw any firm conclusions.

Other complex roundhouses may also have been built in the centuries before 200 BC. The complex roundhouse at Jarlshof in Shetland, for example, is undated, but in the structure that replaced it (an 'aisled roundhouse') both saddle and rotary querns were found. Since saddle querns were apparently replaced by the more efficient rotary querns in Atlantic Scotland around 200 BC, this suggests that the 'aisled roundhouse' was in occupation at this time of transition. The implication of course is that the complex roundhouse was earlier still. This rather indirect dating for the complex roundhouse at Jarlshof appears to be supported by new excavation at the neighbouring settlement of Old Scatness, where preliminary indications suggest that a very well-preserved complex roundhouse similarly dates to before 200 BC.

It is not entirely clear why seemingly specialised architectural features like intra-mural cells and stairs should have emerged at this time. Intra-mural cells may have been intended for a range of purposes, perhaps to supply extra space for storage, or to serve specific functions that demanded seclusion or privacy, or possibly just to save on the building materials that a solid wall would absorb. Such features were by no means confined to the roundhouses themselves. At Crosskirk, for example, intra-mural cells were built into various outworks and external buildings. Whatever their precise function, architectural features of this kind had now become part of the general repertoire of the vernacular stone-building traditions of the region.

Howe of Howe: a roundhouse exposed

Perhaps the best understood complex roundhouse settlement is that at Howe of Howe, near Stromness in Orkney, which was excavated shortly after the completion of work at Bu. Howe represents the most complete excavation of a broch settlement yet attempted, and the later structures on the site will be discussed more fully in chapter 5. What is important here, however, is the light it sheds on the early development of broch architecture.

The Iron Age occupation at Howe began with the construction of a small enclosure built over the site of a long-abandoned Neolithic chambered tomb some time around 700-400 BC. Little is known of the structures that may have lain within this enclosure as they had been thoroughly disturbed by later building activity. Some time prior to 400 BC, however, the first Atlantic roundhouse was constructed within the enclosure on the old tomb mound. The dating is imprecise as it is based largely on the radiocarbon dating of two skeletons found in a drain below the collapse of the roundhouse and does not date the construction or occupation of the building. Although very badly knocked around by later rebuilding, this structure appears to have had walls some 4m thick and of the same broad structural type as the other thick-walled Orcadian roundhouses. Following the catastrophic collapse of this roundhouse, which probably resulted from the instability of the old tomb mound, it was replaced by a complex round-house with walls 3.5m thick. The floor of this new building was much better preserved than that of its predecessor, and it was clear that it had been divided by flagstone partitions similar to those at Bu and Crosskirk (**19**). The internal arrangement of rooms was also similar to the situation at Bu – a large, flagged sub-rectangular room formed the northern part of the interior while in the central area there was an earth-floored room with a large hearth and access to several radial compartments. This seems to suggest considerable continuity of domestic arrangements in Orkney over several centuries.

Like Crosskirk, this second roundhouse contained some of the distinctive features of broch architecture, most notably two intra-mural stairs rising within the walls, and two cells opening from the entrance passage. Also like Crosskirk, however, it was clearly never a broch tower in the traditional mould – the two intra-mural cells were open to the interior of the building, breaking up the wall-line in such a way that it would have been impossible to build any significant stone superstructure above them.

Some time around 200 BC–AD 100, this complex roundhouse was itself remodelled. Its walls were encased within new walls up to 6m thick, containing a single intra-mural staircase and a cell built into the north wall. It seems quite likely that this new building was indeed a broch tower.

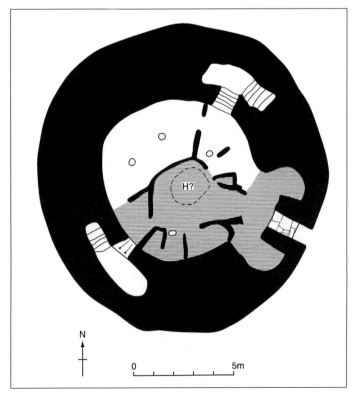

19 *This simplified plan gives one interpretation of the internal arrangements in the complex roundhouse at Howe (Phase 6). The floor was badly damaged so it is impossible to reconstruct with any certainty. The unshaded areas are paved*

Out of Orkney?

So far all of the Atlantic roundhouses we have considered have been found in Orkney and Caithness. As far as the limited evidence allows, we can discern a general development from simple roundhouses like Bu, between 800-400 BC, to more complex roundhouses like Crosskirk perhaps from around 500-200 BC. The date of the first full-blown broch towers is still something of a mystery but it seems likely that they were being built by around 200 BC or thereabouts.

It is tempting to take this simple scheme, which sees a gradual move towards the building of ever more ambitious and complex structures, and apply it to the whole of Atlantic Scotland. We have to remember, however, that it is still based on a tiny number of modern excavations and a pitifully small body of radiocarbon dates. There is no way of proving, for example, that some of the very earliest roundhouses, like Bu itself, did not have upper storeys which have simply not survived. Nonetheless, as a working model it seems to fit the data ^currently available in the north.

This Orcadian sequence cannot, however, be extended uncritically to other parts of Atlantic Scotland. In Shetland and the Western Isles, for example, we have yet to find any likely parallels for the simple Atlantic roundhouses of Orkney, although there are contenders in Argyll. The Atlantic roundhouse settlement pattern in Shetland is, as we shall see in chapter 4, a coherent one, and it may be that most of the known sites were complex roundhouses built around the same time as the excavated examples of Old Scatness and Jarlshof, probably some time before 200 BC.

The Atlantic roundhouses of the Western Isles are a mixed bag. There seems to be far more variability in this region in terms of the shape and size of the buildings and the arrangement of architectural features. In the past this has led many of these sites to be dismissed as 'duns' of uncertain date which made it convenient for archaeologists to ignore them. Survey work during the 1980s in areas such as North Uist and Barra, however, suggested that these rather heterogeneous structures were part of the same phenomenon as the broch towers and shared these island landscapes with them in the second half of the first millennium BC.

Of around 140 Atlantic roundhouses known in the Western Isles, 14 have been at least partially excavated. Without exception, these have proved to be complex roundhouses even where the surface traces were little more than a large pile of rubble. In fact, the site of Dun Bharabhat in Lewis was specifically selected for excavation because of its unprepossessing appearance which did not suggest any level of architectural complexity (**20**). When excavated, however, Dun Bharabhat was revealed as a particularly tiny complex round-house with intra-mural galleries, cells and stairs (**21**). Like Crosskirk, it had clearly never supported a tower-like superstructure and, also like Crosskirk, it had been built in a fairly inept way which led to its premature collapse. Dating

20 *Dun Bharabhat, Cnip, before excavation was a rather featureless mass of collapsed stonework, typical of many Atlantic roundhouses in the Western Isles*

evidence for the site is limited, but secondary occupation within the structure was dated to the first two centuries BC.

In the light of the work at Dun Bharabhat and elsewhere it is difficult to escape the conclusion that simple Atlantic roundhouses, like Bu, were not constructed in the Western Isles in any significant numbers. It may be that architectural complexity was developed more quickly in this region, but it is perhaps more likely that the roundhouse form was only adopted in the west once the traits associated with broch architecture had already emerged.

The impression of variability in design becomes even more marked in Argyll and the Inner Hebrides. Modern excavation of Atlantic roundhouses in this area has been minimal and their chronology remains obscure. It is also difficult to differentiate Atlantic roundhouses in Argyll from some of the later stone forts built by the Scots of Dalriada from the sixth century AD onwards. In some cases, as at the Dalriadic capital of Dunadd, the later builders seem to have rebuilt on the sites of Iron Age roundhouses, but elsewhere they probably constructed entirely new buildings in a similar style.

Of the Iron Age structures which have been excavated in Argyll, the most important is the complex roundhouse of Dun Mor Vaul on Tiree. The interpretations of the radiocarbon dates from this site, however, have been the subject of some controversy and their margins of error are now realised to be so wide as to greatly restrict their value. Single radiocarbon dates from other excavated sites, notably Dun Ardtreck and Dun Flodigarry, both in Skye, also

21 *On excavation, it was quickly revealed that the mass of stone at Dun Bharabhat concealed a complex structure with galleries and intra-mural stairs*

cover broad ranges and do not really help to address the issue of Atlantic roundhouse chronology in any detail. Some of the objects found in Gordon Childe's 1930s excavations at the Atlantic roundhouse of Rahoy, in Morvern, however, do suggest a fairly early date of occupation. A socketed iron axe in a form which clearly mimics earlier bronze versions should date to the very beginning of the Iron Age, perhaps around 700-600 BC. Later occupation is also attested by a continentally-inspired brooch, a La Tène type suggesting occupation in the third century BC.

Although well-dated examples are still few, there is no reason to doubt that sites like Crosskirk, Howe, Old Scatness and Dun Bharabhat are broadly representative of the hundreds of unexcavated Atlantic roundhouses in Caithness, Orkney, Shetland and the Western Isles respectively. It seems reasonable, therefore, to suppose that variations on the complex roundhouse theme had become a common feature of the landscapes of Atlantic Scotland by the middle of the first millennium BC. It was from this background that the broch towers appeared.

3

ANATOMY OF
A BROCH TOWER

We will never know for certain quite when the first broch tower was built. Most probably they emerged from the well-established tradition of vernacular architecture represented by the Atlantic roundhouses some time in the second half of the first millennium BC. Although it is usually assumed that broch towers would have appeared at the end of the Atlantic roundhouse tradition, there is little actual evidence for this. The few unambiguous broch towers which survive as standing monuments have not been excavated in modern times and we have little evidence as to their dates of construction. Only five are known to survive to close to their original height: Mousa in Shetland (13.3m), Dun Carloway in Lewis (9.2m), Dun Troddan and Dun Telve on the mainland opposite Skye (7.6m and 10m respectively), and Dun Dornaigil in Sutherland (6.7m). Any others which once stood so tall may now be unrecognisable after centuries of stone-robbing, decay and erosion.

A ground-breaking statistical analysis of broch architecture was published by Angus Graham in 1947 using a sample of just over 500 sites which he regarded as brochs, or possible brochs, based on the published literature of the time. Although we would now expect that a significant proportion of these sites are likely to have been simple or complex Atlantic roundhouses covering a wide range of structural variation, Graham's work is still enormously useful, especially for the better preserved broch towers where only very limited new evidence has since come to light. In this chapter, we will concentrate on trying to reconstruct how broch towers and other complex roundhouses might have functioned as buildings using the evidence amassed by Graham and the data subsequently added through modern excavation and field survey (**22**).

wall voids

intra-mural
gallery

entrance to stairs

scarcament ledge

22 *This view of the interior of Dun Carloway highlights some of the main features of broch architecture*

Broch architecture

Shape and size

Atlantic roundhouses, despite the name, are not all strictly circular buildings. Their builders often had to adapt their basic design to the eccentricities of the available site, which might be an irregular rocky knoll or a cramped islet which did not allow for a truly circular foundation (**23**). On other occasions, the site might have been already occupied by the ruins of earlier buildings, such as the collapsed chambered tomb under the roundhouses at Howe discussed in chapter 2. As a result, Atlantic roundhouses come in a variety of sub-circular, oval and even sub-triangular shapes, although circularity seems to have been the desired objective where it could be achieved. What seems to have been most important is that the buildings had to be sufficiently regular in shape to allow for roofing. While a certain leeway was possible for the shape of Atlantic roundhouses in general, the tallest of them would have required a more regular foundation, as close to a circle as possible, for maximum stability. As we might expect, the surviving broch towers, such as Mousa, are closer to perfect circles than most.

There is also considerable variation in the size of Atlantic roundhouses. In Orkney alone, the overall diameters vary from 12m to as much as 23m and the internal diameters from around 7m to nearly 14m (a fourfold difference in the size of the enclosed area). Clearly there was no single blueprint for the construction of these structures and, even among the well-preserved broch towers, no two are exactly alike in size, design or layout.

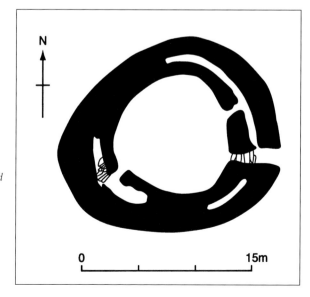

23 *Many complex roundhouses, like this example at Dun Vulan in South Uist, were irregular in shape and could not have achieved the tower-like proportions associated with sites like Mousa. They were, nonetheless, still substantial buildings in their own right. After Parker Pearson, M., Sharples, N.M. & Mulville, J., 1999, figure 1.2*

N

0   15m

Height

The original height of broch towers has been a subject of long-running debate. Essentially there are two views. The first holds that broch towers like Mousa and Dun Carloway are simply the best-preserved examples of what were orig-inally many hundreds of tower-like structures. The second view, originated by Lindsay Scott in the 1940s, holds that the surviving broch towers were always exceptionally tall, and that the vast majority of Atlantic roundhouses would have been of comparatively modest height. The relatively recent discovery of the early simple Atlantic roundhouses and low-walled complex roundhouses like Crosskirk, has tended to lend weight to Scott's ideas. Yet we are still a long way from being able to determine what proportion of Atlantic roundhouses origi-nally stood as broch towers. Indeed the question is unlikely ever to be resolved to everyone's satisfaction since the most important evidence is, by its very nature, missing. However, there are some clues from the surviving structures.

If a significant proportion of the ruined Atlantic roundhouses found dotted around the landscape today were originally broch towers like Mousa, then we might expect that the proportions of these other structures should, where they can be measured, accord broadly with those of Mousa itself. This, however, is far from the case. A series of analyses carried out by Noel Fojut, for example, have shown that Mousa is quite atypical of Atlantic roundhouses in Shetland (24). Of all the known sites, Mousa has both the smallest internal diameter and the smallest external diameter. More important, however, is the extraordinary 'massiveness' of its wall. The ratio between the width of the walls and the overall diameter of a roundhouse (the wall base percentage) has sometimes been taken as a key indicator of original height, the theory being that the taller the original wall, the greater the wall base percentage required to support it. The wall base percentage of Mousa, at 64.5 per cent, is the greatest of any Atlantic roundhouse known: in other words much more of the ground plan of Mousa is taken up by wall foundation than was the case for any other compa-rable structure. This in turn means that the ground plan set out by the builders of Mousa was far better suited to building a tall, tower-like structure than that of any other Atlantic roundhouse in Shetland or indeed Scotland as a whole.

This analysis of the structural characteristics of Mousa suggests two possible scenarios. It may be that there were originally many tall broch towers in Shetland of which only Mousa, being the most stable, managed to survive to modern times. Alternatively, it may be that Mousa was, as its ground plan suggests, always exceptional and may have been substantially taller than any of its contemporaries.

When the study of wall base percentages is extended to other regions, it reveals a high degree of variation. Along the west coast and in the Western Isles, for example, Atlantic roundhouse walls tend to be thinner in relation to overall diameter, perhaps suggesting rather lower structures than their more massively built northern counterparts. We must be wary of pinning too much

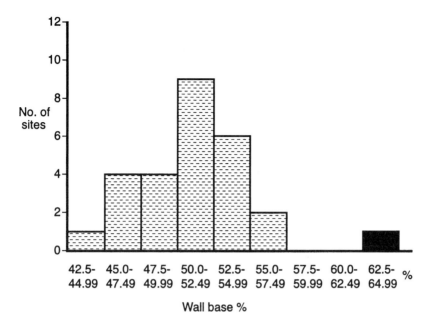

24 *This table shows the wall base percentage of the 27 best preserved Atlantic roundhouses in Shetland. The figure is reached by calculating how much of the overall diameter of building is taken up by the wall foundations. As is clear, Mousa (in black) is set apart from the others as by far the most massively built of the Shetland examples.* After Fojut, 1981, 223

faith in these analyses, however, as we have already seen in chapter 2 that some northern roundhouses, such as Bu and Crosskirk, had their walls episodically thickened. In these cases, the final figure for the wall base percentage will be irrelevant with regard to original height. If, as seems likely, this tendency to build up the thickness of the walls over time was a fairly common feature in the north, it may help explain the apparent discrepancy in wall base percentages between the north and west parts of Atlantic Scotland.

Although Mousa may have been an exceptionally, perhaps uniquely, tall structure, we must not lose sight of the fact that all broch towers and indeed Atlantic roundhouses in general would have been imposing structures in their own right. Even if they did not reach the height of Mousa, many may have been in the 5-10m bracket, which would have been impressive enough in a region where nothing like them had been seen before. The inward batter of the external walls of the best preserved broch towers creates an impression of soaring height, especially when viewed from ground level. It should be remembered, however, that there is not one single broch tower that is taller than it is wide, which one might assume to be a reasonable definition for a tower. That we continue to think of them as such is testament to the visual power they retain even today.

The hollow wall

One of the most instantly recognisable traits of broch architecture is the presence of galleries superimposed within the walls (**colour plate 7**), although the proportion of Atlantic roundhouses in which such features actually survive is surprisingly low. Indeed, Angus Graham was able to point to only 29 structures (from his overall sample of 512) where a first-floor gallery was preserved, and only six where there was evidence for a second or higher storey.

The best preserved examples are, not unexpectedly, those at Mousa where there are six superimposed galleries each large enough for an adult to pass along. All are accessible from the stair and were thus potentially available as storage or sleeping space if required. Once again, however, Mousa seems to be unusual, if not unique. For example, while the lower two galleries at Dun Telve can be comfortably negotiated, and are carefully faced internally, the upper galleries are so constricted and irregularly faced that it is impossible for an adult to pass along them. The same applies to the topmost gallery at Dun Carloway where the inner and outer walls seem almost to converge due to the batter of the outer wall, and where one passage is partly blocked off by slabs which run between the inner and outer wall. In other Atlantic roundhouses there seem to have been galleries with no obvious means of access, which were presumably not used during the day-to-day occupation of the building.

With the possible exception of Mousa, therefore, it seems that the intramural galleries of broch towers were not intended for day-to-day use. Instead, some other purpose must have been intended. One suggestion has been that they provided access to the walls for masons while construction was in progress, thus avoiding the need for scaffolding in areas where timber was notably scarce. This idea might explain why many are apparently inaccessible, since they would have become redundant on completion of the building works, but it does not help explain the narrow, impassable galleries at sites like Dun Telve and Dun Carloway which would have been equally useless for access during or after construction. As an alternative, it is possible that the principal purpose of the galleries was to economise on the amount of stone required to construct these buildings and to reduce the weight of stonework in the upper levels of the tower. Thus the galleries, with their finely-tuned channelling of weight stresses, would have enabled increased height without undue loss of stability.

As well as continuous intra-mural galleries, the walls of some Atlantic roundhouses also contain one or more cells in their basal levels, entered from the interior of the building. The number and disposition of these cells is extremely variable and there was clearly no standard design. Their size and shape also vary enormously suggesting that their function may have been equally varied. Where the roofs of these cells survive they tend to be corbelled, often to a height which would allow an adult to stand upright at least in the central part of the cell.

There is a clear geographical divide between those Atlantic roundhouses where intra-mural galleries begin only at first-floor level, although there may be one or more cells in the basal storey (the 'solid-based' type), and those where the continuous galleries begin at the base (the 'ground-galleried' type). There are also 'transitional' forms where the lower wall may contain an assortment of intra-mural cells and/ or short lengths of gallery. The ground-galleried examples occur predominately on the west coast and in the Western Isles, although a few prominent northern sites, such as Gurness and Midhowe, also have this feature. It has long been recognised that basal galleries seem to have created instability, resulting in the premature collapse of many of these buildings. This has suggested to some, notably Euan MacKie, that ground-galleried structures are on the whole earlier than those with solid-bases (on the principal that we should expect expertise in the building of tower-like structures to improve rather than decline over time). Others would simply regard the two forms as overlapping regional variants. It could also be argued that the use of basal galleries may reflect an over-ambitious development of the hollow-walled building technique at a fairly late stage in its development. Until more sites are excavated to produce strong sequences of radiocarbon dates, such questions are unlikely to be resolved.

Intra-mural stairs

In broch towers where preservation is sufficiently good, the intra-mural spaces usually contain one or more flights of stone steps rising between the walls, linking the galleries at various levels (**25**). Only at Mousa does a spiral stair run clockwise all the way up through the galleried walls to give access to the wall-head (**colour plate 12**). More usually the flights of stairs between galleries are linked by level stretches of gallery space. In many cases, for example at Dun Carloway, access to the stairs is from one of the cells at ground level. This is by no means the only arrangement, however, and quite often the position of stair entries presupposes the former existence of timber fittings. At Gurness and Midhowe, for example, the stairs are accessed from landings well above the ground floor, suggesting that initial access was by timber steps or ladders.

The existence of these stairs may imply that access to the upper galleries was sometimes intended, but it does not really help resolve the question of their function. It may be, for example, that the greatest use of the intra-mural stairs was made during the construction of the building when they might have made it easier to haul stonework to the upper courses. The stairs rarely show any signs of wear such as we would commonly expect to see on the well-used stone steps of more recent historic buildings, and it seems improbable that they were used much for day-to-day access. Aside from intra-mural stairs there are occasionally other forms of access between floors which may have been used more routinely. At Crosskirk, for example, where the intra-mural stair was narrow, badly finished and showed no signs of wear, a stone 'ladder' recessed into the

25 *Intra-mural stairs at Loch na Beirgh, Lewis. The ranging pole lies on the short landing which gives access, through the entrance in the inner wall, to what would have been a timber first floor within the broch tower. The lower steps descend into the unexcavated deposits filling the ground-floor gallery, while the upper steps would presumably have led to the now vanished second floor*

inner wall would have allowed more direct access to an upper timber floor. Elsewhere, there may well have been timber ladders and stairs of which no recognisable trace now survives.

The entrance passage

In the vast majority of cases, Atlantic roundhouses have only a single entrance, a feature they seem to share with timber roundhouses in other parts of Britain. The entrance passages are usually comfortably wide, perhaps around 1.2m, and seldom less than around 0.8m. This may reflect the need to allow access for animals, since most Iron Age beasts, being substantially smaller than their modern counterparts, could have negotiated these passages fairly easily. Their length is obviously dependent on the width of the walls but is seldom less than around 3m. In a handful of instances, mainly in Caithness and Shetland, there are Atlantic roundhouses with more than one entrance, the best known being Clickhimin in Shetland. In each of these cases, however, the additional entrances most likely reflect secondary modification of the original building.

As the only point at which the outer wall is pierced, the entrance passage inevitably creates a potential weak point in the structure. As a result, considerable attention was paid to the selection of good quality lintels to bear the weight of stone above these openings. Sometimes, most notably at Dun Dornaigil in Sutherland, the builders elaborated a little on this theme by employing massive triangular stones which would have served to divert the weight stresses away from the vulnerable entrance passage, as well as creating an imposing façade to greet the visitor (**colour plate 10**).

As with any building, the architecture of Atlantic roundhouses tends to dictate the body position and movement of inhabitants and visitors alike. Entering along the passage into a broch tower like Dun Carloway, most adult visitors would have been required to stoop slightly, bowing their heads, rising and straightening only once inside the building. In this way, the architecture of the passage heightens the sense of transition from outside to inside and accentuates the sense of space within the building. Other aspects of entrance design may also have had cultural rather than practical significance. For example, in Iron Age Britain in general there is a marked tendency for roundhouse entrances to face more or less east. This was traditionally regarded as relating to practical considerations such as the need for shelter from prevailing winds. Recent work, however, has suggested that the preferred easterly orientation is replicated over wide areas of the country with little regard for local wind conditions or topography. Using ethnographic comparisons, archaeologists such as Alastair Oswald have suggested that the easterly orientation may reflect deep-rooted religious ideas related to the rising of the sun in the east. Indeed they have also suggested that many other aspects of the organisation and use of Iron Age roundhouses were structured with reference to the cosmology of the inhabitants who may have seen the roundhouse as the symbolic centre of their world.

Mike Parker Pearson has applied this model to Atlantic Scotland noting that the builders of some broch towers seem to have reversed the usual pattern by adopting a westerly orientation which may, in his view, indicate some special status for these buildings. It is indeed the case that Atlantic roundhouse orientations seem to vary from the expected pattern seen across the rest of Britain, and some of the most impressive structures do indeed fit this model. The entrance at Mousa, for example, faces due west. Of the two most elaborate broch towers in Lewis, however, Dun Carloway faces west-north-west while Loch na Beirgh faces due east. Although much work remains to be done on this particular facet of layout and siting, it is clear that the orientation of these buildings is far from random and would repay closer scrutiny.

Doors and 'guard cells'

Many Atlantic roundhouses have quite detailed evidence for the original position and configuration of the timber doors which would have shut off access along the entrance passage (26 & **colour plate 11**). The location of the door is usually represented by recesses in the wall which would have acted as door checks, or by projecting slabs of stone. Behind the door checks, open slots in the walls of the passage often acted as bar-holes, where a stout wooden beam would have been inserted to hold the door shut. More rarely a socket-stone or pivot-stone in the original floor will show how the timber door would have swung inwards.

The position of the door varies a good deal, but often it is recessed towards the inner end of the entrance passage. This may simply have been intended to provide some shelter for the door, but it has also been suggested that setting the door partway down the passage may have been a defensive feature which prevented attackers from taking a run at it with a battering ram. However, it may equally be the case that a recessed door actually assisted attackers who, once safely ensconced in the outer part of the entrance passage could have adopted a leisurely approach to setting fire to the door. Whatever the defensive merits or demerits, it is clear that the recessing of the door is not a late development as the door in the early roundhouse at Bu was set well down the passage.

As well as provision for a timber door, a great number of Atlantic roundhouses also have 'guard cells' positioned partway along their entrance passages, often paired on either side. The term itself has always been a little contentious since it implies a clear defensive purpose. Although in some cases the wooden beam that barred the main door would have been operated from the guard-cell, it is hard to see how a more active defensive function could have been maintained. The low and cramped entrances to these cells, for example at Dun Carloway, would have severely hampered the movement of any defender until they had squeezed themselves into the entrance passage proper. Some archaeologists have suggested that these cells may have been little more than dog

1 *Clickhimin, Shetland: one of the most important broch excavations of the twentieth century*

2 *Mousa, Shetland: the archetypal broch tower*

3 *Dun Cuier, Barra*

4 *Dun Carloway, Lewis: the partial collapse of the broch tower reveals the inner structure of the walls*

5 *Loch na Beirgh broch tower, Lewis: before excavation this structure was visible only as a low mound in a boggy field*

6 *Clickhimin: the blockhouse, seen from the ruins of the broch tower walls*

7 *Dun Telve, Glenelg: the detail of the wall construction can clearly be seen where parts of the wall have fallen away*

8 *Dun Telve: the interior wall displays the familiar features of broch architecture*

9 *The broch tower of Mousa dominates the small island. This view shows the island of Mousa from mainland Shetland. The broch tower is visible between the two central telegraph poles on the near horizon*

10 *Dun Dornaigil, Sutherland: a detail of the distinctive triangular lintel over the entrance*

11 *Carn Liath, Caithness: a view out through the entrance showing the checks for the wooden door*

12 *Mousa: a view looking up the internal stairs*

13 *Dun Carloway in its landscape context*

14 *Dun Beag, Skye in its landscape*

15 *Dun Loch Druim an Iasgair, Benbecula: an Atlantic roundhouse set on an inaccessible islet, typical of many in the Hebrides*

16 *Dun na Kille, Barra: built into the corner of a modern cemetery, this well-preserved Atlantic roundhouse escaped detection until quite recently*

17 *Gurness, Orkney: the internal stone furniture*

18 *Dun Cuier, Barra: although the interior of this complex roundhouse is clogged with rubble, the scarcement ledge is clearly visible*

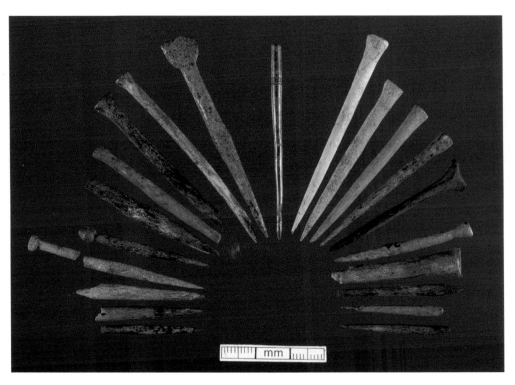

19 *Typical finds: a selection of bone pins from the broch tower at Loch na Beirgh, Lewis*

20 *Dun Telve seen from neighbouring Dun Troddan*

21 *An iron spade-shoe from Cnip wheelhouse in Lewis, dating to the first century AD. The spade rather than the plough was the main cultivation implement in the area until recent centuries. A similar one was recovered from the southern broch of Leckie in Stirlingshire*

22 *Gurness, Orkney: the archetypal broch village*

23 *Jarlshof, Shetland, from the air: the broch tower forms part of a long-lived settlement from the Bronze Age to the medieval period*

26 *The view looking out through the paved and lintelled entrance to the blockhouse at Ness of Burgi in Shetland shows the well preserved rebate and slab-built door checks for the former wooden door*

kennels, store rooms, or places to hang wet clothes and boots, and the non-defensive interpretation is given credence by the rare occasions where the guard cell entrance is apparently set outside the timber door. Their ubiquity and general regularity, however, suggest that they served some fairly basic function for the inhabitants of these buildings. Angus Graham calculated that around a quarter of his sample had no cells, while another quarter had paired cells. Where there was only one, it was usually, but not always, on the right of anyone entering the building.

The most complex set of entrance features yet known occurs at the East Broch of Burray in Orkney, where an inner timber door was secured by a wooden bar set into two deep bar-holes. Beyond this were two opposing 'guard cells' and, still further along the passage, an outer timber door. Whether for defence or simply to control and formalise access to the building, a great deal of care clearly had been taken in the design of this particular suite of entrance features.

Scarcement ledges

Another of the most characteristic features of well-preserved Atlantic roundhouses is the scarcement ledge, projecting from the inner wall to form a circuit around the interior (**colour plate 18**). Usually these are formed by recessing the wall face above the scarcement, but in some cases the stones of the scarcement may actually project slightly into the interior. One of the most substantial scarcements is that in the Loch na Beirgh broch tower in Lewis, which forms a ledge 30cm wide. On occasion there are stone corbels projecting from the scarcement or elsewhere in the wall circuit, which also seem to have served some structural purpose.

Most scarcements seem to occur at heights of between 1.4m and 3.9m, the average being around 2.4m, which would place them comfortably above head height. Traditionally they have been regarded as support mechanisms either for upper floors or roofs, and this does generally seem by far the most likely interpretation, even if the mechanics of the associated joinery remain subject to debate. Occasionally, as at Casteil Grugaig in Lochalsh, the scarcement is so low over parts of the sloping interior (down to 0.7m), that it probably supported a hung floor.

Archaeologists have long pondered the various mechanisms by which a timber floor could be set in place using the support provided by a scarcement ledge. Scarcements in other types of building are features used to support the ends of timber planks or beams and this seems a reasonable suggestion for the purpose of broch scarcements. Angus Graham long ago pointed out the improbability, in a largely treeless region, of beams up to 12m or so in length stretching across the inner spans of the larger broch towers and resting at each end on the scarcement. His suggestion was that a framework of posts set chord-wise might have formed the basic support. In other words, say four timbers might have been laid across parts of the circuit, each end resting on the scarcement to form a square framework on which the floor would be set. In a broch tower with an inner diameter of 10m, this technique would reduce the length of the longest timbers needed from 10m to around 7m. Using a six or eight-sided framework would have let the builders get away with even shorter timbers, though perhaps at the expense of structural stability. Six stone corbels set into the scarcement ledge at Mousa might suggest the use of a six-sided frame, while similar corbels could have supported a four-sided frame at Culswick, also in Shetland.

A few better-preserved sites have multiple scarcements suggestive of upper timber floors. Mousa, for example, has scarcements at 2.1m and 3.8m (the limited space between them suggesting that at least one probably supported a mezzanine rather than a complete floor). Dun Telve also has two scarcements, the upper being some 9m above the ground floor and presumably associated with the roof rather than any high level flooring. Its near neighbour, Dun Troddan, may also have had a high second scarcement, as an early engraving of the site by Pennant seems to depict a now lost scarcement much higher than the surviving one. There are other inconsistencies between his drawing and the surviving features of the building, however, and it is possible that he may have confused the features of the two sites. Dun Carloway survives to more than 9m in height without any trace of an upper scarcement, so we cannot be sure that all broch towers originally had such a feature.

In some cases there is a clear relationship between the scarcement position and openings into the first-floor galleries which seem to indicate beyond reasonable doubt the former existence of a timber floor. At Loch na Beirgh in Lewis, for example, an intra-mural stair from the ground floor leads up to a landing which gives access through a door into the interior of the broch tower at scarcement level (**25**). Turning right a few steps across the presumed timber floor would have allowed entry through a second door into the first-floor gallery.

Wall voids

One of the most intriguing features of the better preserved broch towers is the frequent presence of vertical rows of window-like holes in the inner wall face (**27**). These wall voids look superficially like ladders with improbably wide-spaced rungs. On occasion they are set above entrances to cells or galleries and in such cases they may thus have acted to reduce the weight of stone over these vulnerable points. In other instances, however, they have no such role, and one of the rows at Mousa appears to be purely for show as, apart from the lowest one, they do not even penetrate the inner wall. Indeed, wall voids seem to have created points of weakness in the structure forming 'fault-lines' within the walls. The suggestion that they may have acted to provide some light to the intra-mural galleries seems a rather inadequate explanation for such architectural risk-taking, particularly if the galleries themselves were rarely used. As we shall see below,

27 *This view of Dun Telve, Glenelg, shows not only a very fine vertical row of superimposed wall voids, but also a high level scarcement near the top of the surviving masonry*

however, a recent reinterpretation of broch architecture has suggested a more plausible function for these otherwise inexplicable oddities of design.

Roofs

There seems little reason to doubt that broch towers, like other substantial roundhouses, were fitted with roofs to keep out the wind and rain and to retain heat. The long-held belief that they were bare masonry towers, open to the elements, derived from the traditional but unfounded view that they were essentially defensive refuges rather than settlements and that the inhabitants would thus be content to make do with cramped accommodation in the wall galleries and cells. Over many years, archaeologists have attempted to establish how these buildings might have been roofed and four main variants have emerged.

1. The stone roof: Although some archaeologists, including Angus Graham himself, have toyed with the idea that broch towers might have been roofed entirely in stone, this interpretation can be disposed of fairly quickly. Certainly no standing broch tower gives any hints that the upper walls would ever have

converged to form a stone dome, and no excavated site has provided evidence
for the collapse of such a structure. Moreover, it seems extremely improbable
that the vast weight of a stone roof could ever have been borne on the walls
of a broch tower.

2. The partial roof: In his early twentieth-century excavations at Dun Troddan,
Alexander Curle identified a ring of post-holes more or less concentric with
the inner wall face. This suggested to him that a roof had once been supported
on internal timber posts. The form of roof that Curle had in mind, however,
was a rather peculiar one. He envisaged that only the peripheral space within
the broch tower would have been roofed over. This would have used sloping
timbers which ran down from the scarcement, with their inner ends resting on
the ring of internal posts (**28**). The centre of the building, in Curle's view,
would have been left open to the elements, allowing light to enter.

Curle's reconstruction did not, however, receive universal support. Angus
Graham suggested that rather than a roof at this level there might have been a

28 *The monopitch or*
'bicycle-shed' form of roofing
was once popular with
archaeologists but is now seen
to be highly improbable

'balcony or gangway for traffic', with the actual roof placed higher up. As Graham rightly pointed out, the scarcement at Dun Troddan is only around 2m above the floor, so even a very gently sloping roof would have left almost no headroom for the inhabitants.

A further variant on the partial roof was proposed by Hamilton in the context of his work at Clickhimin. Instead of Curle's low, verandah-style roof sloping inwards into the interior, Hamilton proposed a high roof, set directly on the wall-head, but still leaving the centre of the building open to the elements. There are strong practical objections, however, to the idea that broch towers were only partially roofed. Any large aperture in the roof would have allowed rain and snow to penetrate the centre of the building and would have exposed the inhabitants to the full rigour of the Atlantic Scottish winter. Internal timber fittings would have been vulnerable to rot, and a central hearth would be impossible to maintain in all but the calmest and driest weather conditions. Given that their ancestors had been building warm, secure and fully-roofed roundhouses in timber and stone for many centuries, it is hard to believe that the broch-builders would have exposed themselves to these problems.

3. The low conical roof: Most archaeologists now agree that broch towers were fully roofed, with the most likely form being the conical thatched roof familiar from timber roundhouse construction. There is less agreement, however, on how such a roof was integrated with the very specific architectural form of the broch tower. One possible solution is that the rafters were supported by the scarcement ledge at a relatively low level within the building. There are, however, problems with this interpretation. A low roof deep within the tower, for example, would seem ill-suited to shedding rainwater, far less snow, which would inevitably collect in the constricted space between the base of the thatch and the inner broch wall. Furthermore, at some sites, for example Dun Grugaig, the ground floor is so irregular that parts of the scarcement are barely a metre above the natural surface, suggesting that the scarcement supported a timber floor rather than any form of roof. Elsewhere this form of low roofing is seemingly disproved by architectural features, such as wall voids, which occur above scarcement level (i.e. above the level of the supposed low roof). At Loch na Beirgh, for example, it is clear that access between internal doorways at first-floor level was across a now vanished timber floor at scarcement level. Such a reconstruction would be impossible if the roof had rested on the scarcement.

4. The high conical roof: Given the problems associated with the low roofing model, it seems more likely that broch towers were equipped with conical roofs set higher above the interior (**29** & **30**). The single most compelling piece of evidence for this is the basic principle that any functioning domestic

29 *The conical roof of the broch tower may have been supported by a timber wall-plate resting primarily on the inner wall. The outer wall would have prevented the thatch being uplifted by high winds. Like Hebridean blackhouses of more recent times, the thatch would probably have been held down by ropes or netting weighted with stones*

building in an Atlantic Scottish environment should be weathertight. It follows from this that any openings and voids within the walls should be below rather than above the roof. Without this basic provision, a cascade of water would pour down through the wall spaces whenever it rained or snowed. Thus it seems most likely that the roof, as we might expect of any building, should sit at or near the top of the walls.

It seems probable that the roof would have been supported by the upper masonry of the broch tower (the alternative of timber post supports would require timbers of improbable length, stretching from the floor perhaps 13m or more to the rafters). Since no intact wall-head survives, it is impossible to be sure what provisions were made for the attachment of the roof structure. It is possible that most broch towers originally had a high level scarcement which helped support parts of the timber roof. Such a feature, however, survives only at Dun Telve and there are further wall openings above it which suggest that the roof did not necessarily sit at this level. The most likely solution is probably that the roof was supported on the top of the inner wall, with the outer wall rising slightly higher to protect the base of the thatch from uplift by the wind. The downward thrust of the roof structure would thus be primarily supported by the relatively vertical inner wall, with part of the weight stresses channelled out into the battered outer wall. Following the roofing principles of nineteenth-century Hebridean blackhouses, it is likely that the thatch would have been covered by a net held down by stones. The weight of the fully thatched roof would have been considerable and would have placed a great strain on the walls. Nonetheless, of the alternatives on offer this seems the most likely solution to the roofing question. Its viability, however, cannot realistically be assessed until someone attempts a full-scale reconstruction.

30 *This cut-away reconstruction drawing of Dun Carloway gives some flavour of how the broch tower might have been used in its original form with its high conical roof. It shows a ground floor laid out for animal stalling and storage, the main hearth and living quarters on the first floor, and a partial upper floor.* Drawing by Alan Braby

The broch tower as a building

How then did all these architectural features combine to produce a functioning building? Perhaps the most convincing attempt so far to understand
the workings of the classic broch towers is that of the architect John Hope.
Hope's ideas emerged from his re-examination of Dun Troddan and Dun
Telve, carried out as the basis for a planned (but so far unrealised) reconstruction of a broch tower. Since experience suggested that the single most
significant factor in determining architectural form was the weather, Hope
assumed that the extreme cold, wind and wet of the Atlantic Scottish climate
must have been driving forces in the evolution of broch architecture. Hope's
discussions with archaeologists had convinced him that broch towers were
fully roofed, most likely by the high conical roofing method, but the function
of the superimposed galleries and stairs was still unexplained, especially the
rows of wall voids rising up the inner wall. As we have seen, the surviving
upper galleries are usually impassable and cannot have been intended either
for routine access or for the convenience of the masons building the structure.
Perhaps, therefore, their function was associated with the weather-proofing of
the building.

In any solid-walled drystone construction, as Hope pointed out, rain
would tend to be driven deep into the walls by high winds. As a result, water
would run down the internal wall faces, drip into ground-level cells and
collect within the wall core creating a damp, unhealthy environment. By
introducing intra-mural galleries, to form what were in effect 'cavity walls',
the builders could resolve these problems. Instead of reaching the interior of
the building, rainwater would have penetrated only the outer wall, while the
inner wall remained dry. This interpretation also makes sense of a number of
otherwise enigmatic features of broch architecture. The desire to incorporate
wall voids, despite the structural risks involved, becomes explicable as a
means of enabling warm air from the occupied interior to circulate between
the walls keeping the intra-mural space dry. Thus the combination of
galleries and voids acted as a structural device to maintain a warm and dry
environment inside the building (**31**). The inaccessibility of upper galleries
becomes unimportant if their primary purpose was the prevention of damp
and heat loss.

A further aspect of Hope's model concerned the location of the main
domestic space. At several broch towers, there is evidence that the ground floor
was not the main focus of the building. This is particularly obvious at sites like
Dun Carloway, where a large irregular outcrop of rock forms a large part of the
floor, and at Dun Troddan, where the internal stone facings are poorly finished
below the level of the scarcement. At both sites the continuous intra-mural
galleries start at first-floor level. Combining these observations we might suggest
that the main hearth would have rested on a clay or stone base on a timber floor

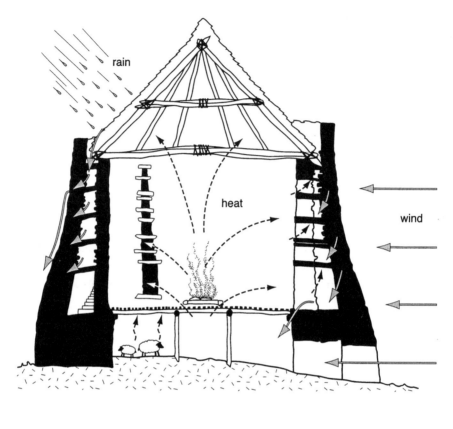

rain

heat

wind

- - - → warm air

⟹ cold air

31 *The diagram shows the basic principles by which broch architecture may have created a warm and dry environment.* Based on ideas proposed by John Hope

at scarcement level, so that the circulation of warm air only became a relevant issue at first-floor level and above. In these buildings the ground floor would probably have been used to shelter stock and this would have contributed in no small way to generating extra heat which would pass up through the floors above. Later occupants may of course have used the ground floor as their main domestic space at a time when the towers were no longer being maintained in their original form. This probably accounts for such features as the sequence of hearths which Curle found inside Dun Troddan.

The Hope model cannot of course be applied as an off-the-peg explanation for all broch towers, far less all Atlantic roundhouses. To begin with, the distinction between ground-galleried and solid-based broch towers introduces an obvious element of variation. It may be that this distinction reflects the position of the main hearth: where it was at ground-floor level, the galleries may have begun from ground-floor level; where the hearth was at first-floor level, the base would have been solid.

More importantly, the most elaborate broch towers were the products of an architectural tradition which had evolved over many centuries. The realisation that intra-mural cavities could prevent the seepage of water might have arisen at an early stage. In early, solid-walled roundhouses like Bu, for example, it would have been difficult to prevent the seepage of water into the entrance passage. Small intra-mural cells in early complex roundhouses like Crosskirk would also have been vulnerable to ingress of water from the overlying wall core. Superimposing additional intra-mural spaces would have resolved this problem without straying far from the existing architectural repertoire. Once the hollow wall construction technique had been developed, its related benefits in terms of economy of materials and enhanced stability would soon have been realised. It is not hard to imagine successive generations of builders attempting progressively higher and more elaborate structures using this basic architectural principle. Hope has suggested that air circulation into the galleries may initially have been through gallery doorways which were subsequently augmented by the more efficient and stylised rows of wall voids. In his view, the builders of the most architecturally developed examples, such as Dun Telve, had refined the techniques of construction to a point where structural integrity was compromised. This need not of course mean that these most impressive broch towers were the last to be built. They may represent little more than a fleeting episode of architectural ambition within a centuries-long development of the vernacular Atlantic roundhouse tradition.

Building a broch tower

John Hope has estimated Dun Telve would originally have contained more than 840m^3 of stone, giving a total weight of perhaps around 2,000 tons. Based on the productivity of modern drystone wallers, somewhere around 400 man-days might have been required for the fitting of the stones to build the broch tower, although this makes no allowance for the lifting of the stones to the upper levels far less the initial quarrying or gathering, transport and scaffold-building. Indeed in the nineteenth century, Captain Thomas estimated, based on his experience of military management, that 60 men would take around 100 days to build a broch tower, assuming that all the material was at hand, in other words some 6,000 man-days exclusive of quarrying and transportation. A figure of 10,000 man-days may be an appropriate scale-order figure for the overall job in other words, 10 people labouring for nearly three years, or 100 people labouring for nearly three months. By any measure, these figures represent an enormous investment of time and labour, particularly since the tasks involved would most likely have required relatively mild weather and would not have fitted particularly conveniently into slack periods in the agricultural cycle. The building of the largest and most elaborate broch towers clearly represented a huge release of labour from the land and the day-to-day business of food production.

Although broch towers survive as stone buildings, we should not forget the large quantities of timber that would have been required in their construction. Their soaring conical roofs, spanning interiors of 12m or more in diameter, would have required long straight timbers as principal rafters. Internal floors, furniture and fittings would similarly have consumed significant quantities of timber in areas where woodland was already a scarce resource. While mainland communities may have had access to relict stands of timber suitable for building, it is most unlikely that plentiful supplies were to be found in any of the main island groups where Atlantic roundhouses are so densely distributed. Although driftwood would have been available in far greater quantities than it is now (since the native woodland along the Atlantic coast of America was at that time intact), the broken and rotted timbers washed up along Scotland's beaches would have been less than ideal for the principal structural elements of such elaborate buildings. While local and driftwood sources would undoubtedly have been exploited, it is probable that access to timber was a key consideration in the construction of broch towers, and it is quite likely that timber would have been imported to the islands from areas richer in surviving woodland. Indeed, the immodest consumption of large quantities of timber may have been as impressive a social statement as the height and massiveness of the broch towers themselves. The sheer volume of resources (stone, timber, labour, skill and time) consumed in the building of a broch tower would have served both to display and enhance the prestige of the inhabitants. The smaller, simpler forms of Atlantic roundhouse would have made similar social statements, but on a proportionately smaller scale.

The professionals

The Atlantic roundhouse tradition was essentially a vernacular building tradition. The skills and knowledge required to build even complex round-houses like Crosskirk and the early structures at Howe could have been held by many within the community and need not have required outside help. Skills in drystone building would have been gained, developed and passed on not just through house-building and maintenance, but also through the routine building and repair of drystone walls and enclosures. Skill levels varied and ambition may sometimes have out-stripped expertise. The inexpert construc-tion of certain Atlantic roundhouses, such as the buttressed and bulging example at Crosskirk and the catastrophically slumped Dun Bharabhat in Lewis, suggest that local skills were often over-stretched by the demands of even relatively low-walled complex roundhouses. Broch towers like Mousa, Dun Carloway and Duns Telve and Troddan, however, were a different matter. The skills required to construct these buildings were of a different order. Indeed, one of the main reasons why the various schemes to reconstruct a broch tower in modern times have foundered is because the drystone-building skills required are simply not available today.

Architects, such as John Hope, who have examined broch towers, have often been adamant in their belief that these were the products of highly-skilled specialists who, if not professional in the modern sense, must have spent a significant proportion of their lives in the learning and practice of broch construction. Archaeologists too, notably Euan MacKie, have also suggested that there may have been a 'caste' of specialist broch architects. As well as the sheer scale and complexity of the best-preserved broch towers, there are subtler indicators of specialist skill. As Hope has noted, several of the largest broch towers encompass elements of tracery walling, where stones are set with the long axes to the wall face rather than set with their long ends bonded into the wall which would have created greater stability. Tracery creates a more regular and elegant wall face, but requires considerable confi-dence and skill to achieve.

Quite how such specialist builders may have organised themselves is uncertain. It is possible that a single specialist could have carried out the skilled elements of design and construction, with the labour being provided by the community especially since, in terms of overall man-hours, the vast majority of the work would no doubt have involved unsophisticated lifting and carrying. To take the estimates of man-days produced by Hope and Thomas, this might suggest that around 400 man-days of specialist labour and an addi-tional 5,600 man-days of unskilled assistance could have been sufficient for a broch tower. In other words, two specialist masons accompanied by 24 unskilled labourers might have built such a tower in 200 days, assuming that the stone had first been gathered.

It is possible to imagine a few individuals based in different regions building to order for locally wealthy families with sufficient resources to support such a project and sufficient desire to display their wealth to all comers. Such broch specialists would have drawn on generations of experience in vernacular drystone building, but may themselves have pushed the boundaries of the architectural form to fulfil the aspirations of their patrons. They may have occupied a social niche analogous to other specialists or semi-specialists in Iron Age society, such as bronze-smiths and iron-workers, perhaps itinerant and landless, or conceivably supported by a permanent patron who might 'lend' them out to supporters and clients. It seems most likely, however, that the great majority of Atlantic roundhouses were simpler structures built in a single season by those who would subsequently inhabit them, perhaps with help drawn from the wider local community or kin-group.

4

BROCH LANDSCAPES,
BROCH PEOPLE

Iron Age landscapes in the north and west of Scotland were similar in many ways to those of the present day. Despite the intervening centuries of peat-stripping for fuel and the aggressive improvement of the peatland fringes to bring more land into cultivation, much of what we see now would have been recognisable to the Atlantic roundhouse builders. The island groups of Orkney, Shetland and the Western Isles in particular would have been open and largely treeless. Pockets of cultivated land, often around the coastal fringes, would have been set within wider areas of rough pasture. Even the north mainland seems to have seen a sharp decline in tree cover during the Bronze Age, with open conditions prevailing around the Atlantic roundhouse of Crosskirk by the middle of the first millennium BC.

The landscapes in which the first Atlantic roundhouses were built had already witnessed several thousands of years of human land use. In Sutherland, for example, Atlantic roundhouses often occupy dominant locations over-looking the grassed-over remains of scattered Bronze Age farms and fields (**32**). Indeed, many of these landscapes had been seriously degraded, partly through generations of intensive and sometimes unsustainable agricultural practices, and partly due to a climatic downturn which had affected the uplands since the latter part of the second millennium BC. Some areas of Bronze Age settlement on the north mainland, as at Lairg in Sutherland, had been abandoned at this time, and throughout much of Scotland there was a retreat of farming communities from the more marginal uplands. In North Uist, settlement seems to have contracted to the coastal belt, abandoning large parts of the interior which had been farmed previously. Throughout the islands, low-lying and coastal areas which could offer a wider range of environmental resources seem increasingly to have become the focus of settlement.

Any contraction in the land available for settlement is bound to have had serious social consequences. Unless population fell in parallel with the diminution in the land's productive capacity, then competition for resources would

32 *The Atlantic roundhouse at Kilphedir in Sutherland forms a dominant presence over the adjacent valley.*
Photograph: RCAHMS

inevitably have increased. The severity of such competition was probably dependent to a large extent on the timescale involved. Settlement contraction over a short period would almost certainly have created major strains within society as dispossessed marginal communities were forced to seek land in already settled areas. In such a situation we might expect conflict, instability and warfare. If, however, the pace of environmental change was slower, perhaps drawn out over several centuries, then the outcome may have been less dramatic. We would still expect to see an increasing concern with the marking of rights to land and resources, and perhaps evidence of competition or conflict between neighbouring communities, but the flow of people from the uplands may have been sufficiently slow that crisis and collapse could be avoided.

It may be in just such a situation that the first Atlantic roundhouses were built, by communities whose access to land and other resources was increasingly insecure. By stamping the presence of the community onto the landscape through the building of a massive stone roundhouse (and even the earliest, simplest of these would have been visually imposing in a landscape where nothing on such a scale had been seen for many centuries), farming communities could stake a clear claim to ownership and control. Over time, the symbolic value of such houses would inevitably increase still further, as concepts of ancestry and identity became intertwined with the visual impact of the structure and its physical dominance of the locality.

Dividing the land

The dense distributions of Atlantic roundhouses in many parts of Atlantic Scotland have encouraged archaeologists to try to understand how Iron Age communities used the land and to examine questions relating to population levels and the reconstruction of prehistoric 'territories'. Any attempt to understand how prehistoric landscapes were divided and farmed has to rely on several assumptions. Firstly, it must be possible to identify a large proportion of the sites that were originally occupied. For most periods and areas in prehistory this would be a forlorn hope. The sheer massiveness of Atlantic roundhouses, however, combined with the relatively low intensity of later land use, makes it likely that a large percentage of the original population of sites have escaped destruction in some areas. Secondly, we must be confident that our sites were occupied at the same time. This is a little more problematic, especially now that the development of Atlantic roundhouses can be seen to extend over as long as 700 years. Nonetheless, we can take some solace from the fact that the great majority of these sites seem to have been inhabited over many centuries (perhaps around 1,200 years or 50 generations in the case of Howe). Even if Atlantic roundhouses within a given area were built over a protracted period, it is a reasonable assumption that their occupation would have overlapped to some extent. Thus it may be possible, in some instances, to glimpse the nature of Iron Age land division and resource utilisation.

The most detailed work along these lines has been Noel Fojut's attempt to establish a 'geography' for the Shetland Iron Age using a range of spatial, locational and statistical techniques. Shetland is perhaps the most amenable part of Atlantic Scotland for this sort of study. A large number of sites are known, occupying most of the likely locations for prehistoric settlement around the coastal fringes of the archipelago. As yet, there are no known simple Atlantic roundhouses in Shetland and none of the late broch villages, so in general the sites seem a relatively homogenous group compared to neighbouring Orkney. Nonetheless, the known sites must represent a minimal view of the original distribution since even in the best surveyed regions some structures will inevitably have been lost to the sea, wholly obscured by modern or medieval buildings, or rendered invisible by stone-robbing and vegetation growth. Fojut estimates that the 75 known sites may represent an original total of not more than 100, and this seems a reasonable working assumption for the region.

In general, and perhaps unsurprisingly, Fojut's analysis showed that Atlantic roundhouses in Shetland were located in those areas where agricultural potential was highest, with relatively good soils and sheltered conditions (**33**). Most had access to arable land, although good quality grazing may have been more important, and most had easy access to the sea. Although some sites may have been selected with defensive considerations in mind, this seems to have been a secondary consideration compared to the availability of good land.

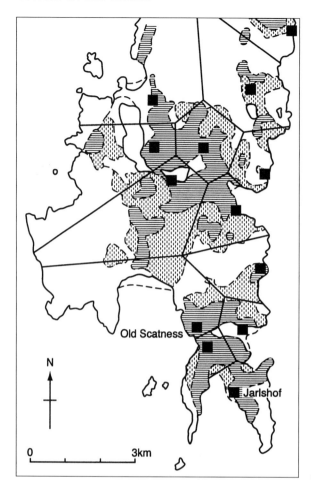

33 *A modified version of Fojut's reconstructed Atlantic roundhouse 'territories' in the southern part of Shetland, showing land of actual (darker) and possible (lighter) arable potential. After Dockrill 2002, 155*

In general, the choice of settlement location takes little account of the presence of neighbouring communities, and there is no sign of the clustering that might be expected if economic activities, such as ploughing or herding, had been carried out in partnership. Indeed, the study seems to demonstrate that Atlantic roundhouse communities in Shetland were essentially self-sufficient units with little need for day-to-day co-operation with their neighbours.

Most of the 'broch territories' examined by Fojut in the southern part of Shetland, where arable land is relatively good, had the capacity to support upwards of 100 people, even in poor years. What we cannot know, however, is how intensively these territories were actually farmed. It may be that similar sizes of population were associated with all of the roundhouses, but that some may have had to work much harder on less amenable land in order to survive. Alternatively, some of the more favourable 'broch territories' may have supported substantial populations, some of whom would presumably have lived in dependent settlements not yet recognised archaeologically. Some of the Atlantic roundhouses in the least promising locations, with little arable and only poor quality grazings, were in areas with access to other resources such as sea-bird nesting sites, from which eggs could have been obtained and perhaps traded.

Studies in the Western Isles, principally in Barra and North Uist, have suggested broadly similar patterns of settlement. Barra and the small islands to the south contain some 18 known Atlantic roundhouses, mostly occupying well-defined natural 'territories' (**34**). This Iron Age settlement pattern covers essentially the same parts of the island occupied in the post-medieval settlement (with the notable exception of the island capital, Castlebay, which only emerged as a fishing centre in the historic period). Population statistics become available for Barra from 1755 onwards, and it is possible to use these figures to highlight some implications of the Atlantic roundhouse settlement pattern. Although the 1755 data cannot be used to indicate prehistoric population figures, they are useful in assessing the implications of some alternative social interpretations of Atlantic roundhouses.

The population figure of 1,150 people living in Barra and its associated islands in 1755 reflects what was more or less a subsistence economy, although the figure had begun to be inflated by the growth of the kelp industry and the

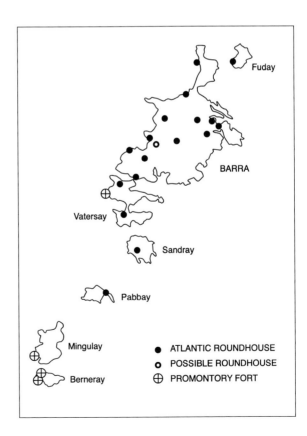

34 *The distribution of Atlantic roundhouses and related structures in Barra and adjacent islands*

commercialisation of fishing. So perhaps around 600-1,000 would be a realistic estimate of the sort of population size that might have been supported by subsistence farming alone. This would give a crude estimate of around 33-55 people associated with each known Atlantic roundhouse 'territory'. A comparable exercise for North Uist gives a figure of 29-49 individuals associated with each of the 51 known Atlantic roundhouses. What is immediately apparent is that an extremely substantial population figure, enormously in excess of that recorded for 1755, would have to be invoked to argue that Atlantic roundhouses had anything approaching the status of tribal centres or élite residences. In fact, the number of known Atlantic roundhouses in both North Uist and Barra is remarkably similar to the number of tenant farmers occupying the same islands during the mid-eighteenth century and well above that of even the most petty aristocracy.

Further insights into the likely population associated with Atlantic roundhouses can be gleaned from examining the small islands south of Barra, several of which have one or two roundhouses. Population records for these islands are vague, but they do at least give the numbers of families present, while from the overall population figures we know that the mean family size was seven individuals. Fuday, Sandray and Pabbay, which each have evidence for one Atlantic roundhouse, were occupied in 1755 by 3-9 families each, i.e. 21-63 individuals. These islands are now wholly uninhabited, and it would be difficult to argue that prehistoric population figures could have been much higher than those of 1755. Indeed Pabbay, with its single Atlantic roundhouse Dunan Ruadh, gives some idea of what the minimum resource base needed to support a roundhouse-building community may have been. The island is around 3km², with a rocky inhospitable coast. It lacks any significant arable land and has no obvious access to any other island which does not have its own roundhouse site. It is stretching credulity then to imagine that Dunan Ruadh was the home of an élite group in any meaningful sense. Perhaps it was built to meet the aspirations of the small island community, two or three families at most, and to mark the legitimacy of their claim to Pabbay and its limited resources.

These studies make it clear that Atlantic roundhouses were not solely the homes of the social élite. There are simply too many of them. Instead they seem to have been the settlement form to which those families who held land aspired. The social status and degree of material comfort enjoyed by these communities may have ranged quite widely. While there may well have been other groups living within these island landscapes, perhaps landless or dependent families, it is hard to find much trace of them archaeologically. Although the variation in the scale and grandeur of the Iron Age buildings, from the simplest low-walled roundhouse to the tallest broch tower, suggests marked variations in status or wealth, each roundhouse-building community seems to have enjoyed a fair degree of autonomy. Their ability and willingness to invest the time, labour and resources required to build and maintain these buildings suggests there was no higher authority to soak up their surplus labour and production. This is in marked contrast to the medieval period in the same region, when the social élite occupied castles and great houses built from the surplus labour and resources of populations whose own modest dwellings are almost wholly invisible archaeologically.

Making a living

The range of economic options available to the communities of Atlantic Scotland would always have been fairly limited. Wherever modern excavation of Atlantic roundhouses has recovered evidence for the Iron Age economy, it has revealed a balance between arable and pastoral farming, with a limited component of fishing and fowling. The specific subsistence regime in any given time and place will always have been constrained by local environmental conditions but, as we shall see, there was still some room for cultural choice and tradition to play a part in determining the balance of the local economy.

Animal husbandry

Throughout Atlantic Scotland, pastoralism would always have been a vital feature of the economy. At Bu, during the early part of the Iron Age, cattle were the most important species, followed by sheep and a small number of pigs. This pattern seems to be replicated throughout the Iron Age on most sites where data is available. Even where sheep outnumber cattle, the much higher meat yield of cattle would usually have made them the dominant species. Occasionally there is evidence of other animals that may have played a subsidiary role, such as the ducks, geese and domestic fowl, recorded at Howe in the last couple of centuries BC.

One of the main areas of disagreement between archaeologists studying the economic basis of the Atlantic Scottish Iron Age concerns the extent to which dairy farming was practised. The high proportion of calf bones in the middens associated with Dun Vulan in South Uist, suggested to the excavators that the inhabitants had practiced a dairying economy in which young calves had been killed off so that milk could be used for human consumption. Since similar patterns have been observed in the faunal assemblages from other sites, this implied that dairying might have been a widespread feature of Atlantic Scottish Iron Age economies. Others, however, have been less convinced. Finbar McCormick, for example, has noted accounts in early documentary sources which suggest that primitive cattle would not yield milk unless stimulated by the presence of the calf. Even as late as the eighteenth century, Martin Martin reported that Hebridean cows could be milked only if their calf was present. Following this argument, the culling of newborn calves would seem to be incompatible with dairying. Instead, McCormick has suggested that the slaughter of these young animals may have been due partly to the difficulties in securing an adequate fodder supply to see them safely through the winter months, and partly to provide a ready source of meat when other resources were scarce. Rather than reflecting a thriving dairy-based economy, the predominance of calf bones in domestic middens would in his view signify an economy under stress.

Documentary records and ethnographic accounts do, however, describe a range of ways in which primitive cattle could be encouraged to produce milk even after the slaughter of their calves. Accounts from Ireland and the Hebrides suggest that placing the skin of the dead calf over a frame and proffering it to the cow could stimulate milk flow. Other methods included 'cow blowing' as recorded by Dinely in Ireland in 1681, which reputedly involved blowing heavily into the 'bearing place' of the cow, at not inconsiderable risk of a 'shitten nose'. Thus it is certainly possible that the communities of Atlantic Scotland could have devised methods to release milk from their cattle while also utilising the meat from the young calves. As yet, however, the argument remains unresolved.

Arable agriculture
Although much of Atlantic Scotland today is devoid of arable agriculture, this has more to do with the economics of modern mechanised farming than with the productivity of the land itself. Until quite recently, subsistence practices in the region relied heavily on arable farming to provide food for the population. Most Atlantic roundhouses excavated under modern conditions have produced evidence for arable agriculture, and even the very earliest excavations describe the discovery of stone querns used for grinding grain into flour. Evidence for arable agriculture now comes from a number of sources such as pollen analysis, carbonised grains from excavated sites, grain impressions on pottery, and from the detailed study of the soils in which crops were grown. Indeed, it has become apparent that huge investments of labour and energy were poured into the painstaking improvement of soils over several millennia. Pioneering work by Steve Dockrill and his collaborators in Orkney and Shetland has shown how infield soils were laboriously improved over many generations by the progressive addition of manure including such materials as domestic midden, ash, seaweed, turf and human waste. Over time, this created localised but extremely fertile patches of infield close to the settlement which could provide high yields of barley, which was the dominant crop throughout the region in prehistory. Recent research has shown that the creation of these man–made or 'plaggen' soils may go back as far as the late Neolithic period making them among the earliest artificially enhanced soils in northern Europe. Once established, these fertile pockets would have proved intensely valuable for successive generations, and their existence may have much to do with the remarkable longevity of particular settlement locations in the islands (**35**). Dockrill has suggested that

35 *Dun Loch an Duin, Shader: a sequence of construction seems to be reflected at this islet-sited Atlantic roundhouse in Lewis. A large stone spread below the water line to the top left of the islet seems to be the remains of an earlier stone building, while the causeway and outline of an earlier 'ghost' islet can be seen to the right.* Photograph: D.W. Harding

this long-established pattern of infield cultivation was intensified still further during the Iron Age, possibly indicating an increasing reliance on arable production during the broch period.

Perhaps one of the major factors in this arable intensification was the adoption of iron which occurred across northern and western Europe during the first half of the first millennium BC. This new metal made available a range of more efficient and effective tools for tilling the land and harvesting the crop. The poor survival properties of iron in most soil conditions, however, make it hard to trace the development of iron technology. Indeed, in Atlantic Scotland the adoption of iron can be inferred more easily from the disappearance of stone agricultural implements than it can from the appearance of iron itself. Nonetheless, iron had almost certainly been adopted in Atlantic Scotland by around 700 BC, which was not substantially later than elsewhere in Britain. There are some further indicators of increased arable production at around this time. Julie Bond has noted that the incidence of burnt grain in domestic buildings increases markedly during the Iron Age and suggests that this may be due to the larger scale processing of crops within houses. Perhaps the best evidence so far retrieved for the storage of barley within an Atlantic round-house comes from the site of Upper Scalloway in Shetland. Associated with the collapsed remains of burnt roofing material was a large quantity of burnt grain which was interpreted as having been stored in the roof space of the building. The increased problem of pest control which would inevitably have resulted from the bulk processing and storage of larger quantities of grain may even account for the speedy introduction of the domestic cat which made its first appearance at sites such as Howe and Old Scatness in the last centuries BC. The introduction of new crops such as flax and most importantly oats, which could grow on ground too marginal for barley cultivation, seems to mark a further intensification of the arable farming economy in the post-broch centuries of the first millennium AD.

Methods of crop processing also became more efficient during the latter part of the first millennium BC. In Atlantic Scotland, as elsewhere, the tradi-tional form of quern, used to grind grain into flour, was the saddle quern, variants of which had been used since the inception of agriculture. The saddle quern was little more than a flattened stone, the upper surface of which was ground into a shallow hollow by the repeated grinding of grain using a hand-held upper stone or rubber. During the Iron Age, a new form of quern was adopted across Europe. The rotary quern comprised two stones, the upper of which was rotated by means of a wooden or bone handle (**36**). Grain was poured through an opening in the upper stone and ground between the two stones. The rotary quern marked a major technological advance on the saddle quern and greatly speeded up the processing of grain into flour. Indeed, small hand-mills of this basic form continued in use into recent centuries in many parts of Scotland.

Wild resources

Throughout Britain, Iron Age economies were based essentially on domesti-cated plants and animals, with little reliance on wild resources, and Atlantic Scotland was no exception. Nonetheless, in a region where agriculture was more than usually vulnerable to small-scale fluctuations in weather and climate, communities with a broadly-based economy which drew on the whole range of naturally available resources would have been far more resilient to environ-mental pressures. It is no surprise then to see evidence for the exploitation of a wide range of wild resources, albeit usually on a fairly limited scale.

Red deer bones and antler fragments are found quite widely on Atlantic roundhouse excavations, suggesting that some small-scale hunting was practised from time to time, but they usually occur as a fairly small component of the animal bone assemblage. On some sites, however, red deer were present in such high numbers that they probably reflect the management of herds

36 *The rotary quern in use.* Drawing: Alan Braby

rather than opportunistic hunting. At Dun Mor Vaul on Tiree, for example, an island which was probably too small and densely occupied to maintain much of a wild herd, red deer made up a substantial proportion of the faunal material. In the Bhaltos peninsula on the west coast of Lewis, faunal assemblages from the broch tower of Loch na Beirgh, the complex roundhouse of Dun Bharabhat, and the wheelhouse of Cnip, together indicate a heavy reliance on red deer spanning around a thousand years from the last few centuries BC to around AD 800. Unlike Tiree, Bhaltos was well-placed to support substantial red deer herds, and these seem to have been at least partly managed by human populations throughout much of prehistory.

While red deer exploitation on any significant scale may have been restricted to a few suitable areas, marine resources were available to the great majority of Atlantic Iron Age communities. Marine mammals such as seals were a valuable source of oil, skins and meat, although this was probably more through the exploitation of dead or stranded animals washed up on the shore than through hunting. The same applies to whales which, as well as oil and meat, yielded large bones which could be put to a variety of structural and craft uses. Fishing was seemingly less important in the Iron Age diet than we might imagine. Most prevalent were immature saithe and related species which could be caught from the shore using nets or lines, and there is little to suggest that deep-water fishing from boats was practised before the Viking period. Wild birds also represented an important supplement to the diet. Over 100 species of bird were recovered from the various phases of settlement at Howe, representing a more or less complete range of the species which would have been found in Iron Age Orkney. Prominent among them are sea-birds, notably the now extinct great auk.

Although the naturally occurring flora of Atlantic Scotland is perhaps less rich than its fauna, there is some evidence for the human use of wild plant resources. Camilla and James Dickson, for example, have recorded a number of unusual charred seeds found in a stone cupboard in the broch tower at Howe, comprising skull-cap, dead-nettle and sheep's sorrel, each of which can be used as herbal remedies. As these plants all grow in different habitats it seems unlikely that their occurrence together was accidental. It has been suggested that they may represent a collection of plants gathered specifically for their curative properties and that the cupboard might have been effectively an Iron Age medicine cabinet. The range of conditions which might be treated using such plants is wide; several have antiseptic properties which could have been used to treat cuts, while others could have ameliorated the effects of rheumatism and diarrhoea.

Wild resources also provided the fuel essential for life in the north and west of Scotland. Charcoal from Atlantic roundhouse excavations is usually fairly sparse, presumably because wood was often too valuable a resource to burn routinely as fuel. More usual was the burning of peat or peaty turf, which was identified at Bu, or materials such as dried dung and seaweed. Driftwood, such as the North American spruce recovered from sites like Howe, may have been a principal source of timber for fuel.

Crafts and exchange

Throughout the Atlantic Scottish Iron Age there is considerable evidence for the local, domestic production of a range of goods. Spindle whorls and distinctive long-handled weaving combs suggest the manufacture of cloth to serve local needs. Similarly, where the soil conditions allow for its survival, the debris of bone and antler-working shows that these activities were routinely carried out within houses. Evidence for metal-working is scarce, although we can be fairly sure that there was local provision for the manufacture and repair of iron agricultural implements. Clay moulds used for casting fine items of bronze, however, become common finds only later, during the early centuries AD.

Mainly as a result of its high survival potential, pottery dominates the finds assemblages for a great many Atlantic roundhouse sites. Variations in the quantity of pottery from area to area and the varying degree to which it was decorated probably relates to deep-rooted differences in the ways in which food was prepared and served. Pottery in the Western Isles, for example, was both more common and more highly decorated than elsewhere throughout the Iron Age, and local traditions of pottery manufacture continued to evolve and develop through the succeeding Viking and medieval periods long after they had ceased elsewhere. The pottery of the last few centuries BC and first couple of centuries AD, coinciding with the period of Atlantic roundhouses and then wheelhouses, was especially finely made and elaborately decorated with incised and applied patterns (**37**). Nonetheless, this pottery was locally made and consisted of entirely hand-built vessels fired on domestic hearths or bonfires. In general it required little specialised technical knowledge, although a few sherds from a late phase at Howe were probably finished on a potter's wheel. Vessel forms at Howe, which provides the best understood assemblage presently available from the north, changed little through the Iron Age with straight-sided and shouldered jars dominant, although a greater variety of

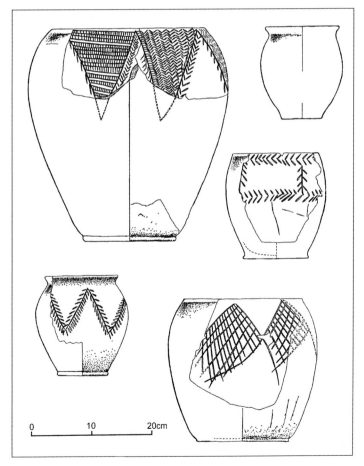

37 *Reconstructed drawings of a selection of pots from Dun Mor Vaul in Tiree.* Based on illustrations in MacKie 1974, 287

forms and more decorated vessels appeared during the broch village period (chapter 5).

Despite its archaeological visibility, pottery may have played only a minor role in some areas. Containers made from wood, leather or basketry may have served similar needs elsewhere. Very rarely, exceptional conditions of preservation allow the recovery of such perishable materials. A small assemblage of waterlogged wood, for example, was recovered from the underwater excavations at Dun Bharabhat in Lewis, while an Iron Age fire at Howe led to the preservation of charred organic objects including a wooden stave bucket and a heather basket.

During the period in which Atlantic roundhouses were being built, there is little evidence of internal trade or exchange. This is perhaps unsurprising given the economic self-sufficiency suggested by the landscape studies considered earlier, yet the spread of broch architecture itself shows that there was a high degree of communication along the Atlantic Scottish sea routes throughout the period. The movement of people from one community to another, most importantly through marriage, would most likely have involved the exchange of gifts, as would the making and sealing of alliances. Such gifts may largely have taken the form of animals, perishable foodstuffs, textiles or furs, and thus be archaeologically invisible. Other materials may also have left no detectable trace. Iron ore, for example, was most probably traded from one region to another though this would be near impossible to identify archaeologically. Locally available foodstuffs, such as seabird eggs and red deer meat, may have been exchanged by certain communities in return for agricultural products. Structural timber may also have been exported, perhaps by mainland communities to the largely treeless islands. The majority of such trade, if it existed, is beyond recovery. There are, of course, occasional exceptions. Steatite, a soft stone found only in Shetland, was used as a tempering agent in some Orcadian pottery, and a vessel made from steatite was found at Gurness. A handled steatite cup found at Dun Troddan, on the west mainland opposite Skye, shows that some such vessels could be passed on even further, although its very uniqueness serves to highlight how unusual this level of exchange must have been. Social links over long distances, for example between island groups, may have been the exception rather than the rule.

Religious life

The absence of formal religious sites is one of the most striking characteristics of Iron Age Britain. Unlike much of continental Europe where cemeteries and elaborate burials are common, the dead are almost absent from the Iron Age landscapes of Britain. It seems most likely that the majority of people were disposed of in ways which left no tangible trace, perhaps through exposure of the corpse to the elements, deposition in rivers, or cremation followed by the scattering of ashes. Instead, the archaeology of the period is dominated by houses, settlements, farms and fields. As a result, archaeologists have often treated British Iron Age societies as practical farming folk of a kind familiar from the more recent rural past. Studies of Iron Age society have consequently tended to focus on rather dry economic issues such as crop yields and trade patterns, and practical matters such as roundhouse reconstruction. However, it has become more apparent over recent years that these societies which have often seemed so familiar were in many respects quite alien to our own experience. Attention has increasingly turned to the less easily explicable elements of Iron Age life, such as the fragmentary or mutilated human remains found in many apparently domestic sites across Britain, and the deposits of humans and animals in disused grain pits at hillforts such as Danebury in Hampshire.

Although there were few cemeteries or specifically religious sites until late in the Iron Age, ritual was by no means absent. Instead of being set apart from day-to-day life, however, ritual and religion were incorporated within the domestic sphere and absorbed within the activities of daily life. Often this involved placing collections of carefully chosen objects within particular parts of the settlement, such as enclosure ditches, entrance areas, post-holes, hearths, or pits under the floors of houses. This sort of 'structured deposition' could range from the dramatic (the burial of human body parts) to the apparently mundane (the burial of pots or joints of meat). Some of the best evidence for such ritualised behaviour in Iron Age Britain has in fact come from Atlantic Scotland where, like so many other aspects of life, ritual and religion appear to have focused more or less exclusively on the house. The best evidence for structured deposition has derived not from Atlantic roundhouses, but from the wheelhouses which succeed them as the standard form of domestic settlement in the Hebrides some time around the first century BC (chapter 7). Structured deposits buried within several Hebridean wheelhouses provide further evidence for the focal role of the house in ritual life. Deposits placed behind the walls of the wheelhouse at Cnip in Lewis, for example, included the fleshed head of a great auk, the articulated backbone of a cow and a complete pottery jar, while a further deposit within the settlement comprised part of a human head accompanied by broken sherds of pottery. Excavation of the wheelhouse at Sollas in North Uist revealed around 150 pits dug into its soft sand floor, of which around 60 contained animal deposits including cattle, sheep and pig. Most dramatic of all, the remains of a child and various young animals were found mixed and divided between four pits under the floor of a fragmentary building at Hornish Point in South Uist. Many such deposits seem to mark the foundation or the closure of buildings, while others may relate to particular events in the life of the community.

These well-preserved ritual deposits all derive from sites on the machair, the alkaline shell sands which fringe the western coasts of the Western Isles. Soil conditions there have led to the exceptional preservation of bone deposits which would otherwise have decayed. Unfortunately, most Atlantic round-houses lie in acidic soils, where bone preservation is poor, so similar deposits are unlikely to have survived. There are, however, some hints that the ritual deposits of the Hebridean wheelhouses may reflect more widespread traditions. A human hand, for example, was found in the midden under the outer skin of roundhouse walling at Bu: not the sort of thing to be lost accidentally. More striking still, the remains of a teenage boy and a woman in her twenties were discovered in a drain below the entrance passage to the complex roundhouse at Howe. Other human remains from the same period of this site's use included a disproportionate number of skull and jawbone fragments, suggesting that heads were preferentially selected for deposition within the settlement.

Several Atlantic roundhouses seem to have been used for burial after aban-donment or during the period when the settlement was in decline. Since conventional burial seems to have been exceptional in the Iron Age it may be that these burials were of special importance or contained individuals that were in some way marked out for special treatment. Late in the Iron Age occupa-tion at Crosskirk, for example, an extraordinary burial was placed in the floor of a building adjacent to the roundhouse. This comprised a cist or box-like structure of stone slabs, projecting well above the floor, into which was placed the body of a well-built elderly or middle-aged man who had been crippled by arthritis. The corpse was placed in a seated position with his back to the hearth, facing out to sea to the prominent rock stack known as the Old Man of Hoy. The building was then seemingly burnt down, perhaps as part of the funeral ritual.

The religious beliefs and practices of these Iron Age communities were undoubtedly rich and complex, and we are still some way from achieving any real understanding of them. What is clear, however, is that the house was the heart of the community and the focus for religious as well as physical life.

5

LORDS OF THE NORTH

In some parts of Atlantic Scotland, such as the Western Isles and Shetland, patterns of settlement characterised by scattered farming communities, each working their own patch of land, remained in place throughout much of the Iron Age. Although some broch towers, like Dun Carloway or Mousa, stood out as grander than their neighbours, there is little evidence for any sort of social hierarchy. In Orkney, however, things were different.

Howe: from roundhouse to village

Some time in the last few centuries BC, the settlement at Howe in Orkney underwent a dramatic transformation. The older buildings, comprising the complex roundhouse described in chapter 2 and a few outbuildings, were dismantled and largely cleared away, leaving only the stubs of the roundhouse wall which were encased within those of an entirely new roundhouse. The massive wall base of this latest building (occupying some 62.5 per cent of its overall diameter) was close to the proportions of Mousa, suggesting that it was almost certainly a broch tower. Even more striking, however, was the redesign of the associated settlement. What had previously been a motley collection of outbuildings was replaced by a highly organised 'village' of six houses clustered within the surrounding rampart and ditch (**38**).

The layout of the Howe broch village conveys a sense of formal organisation, although its full expression was limited by the small space and awkward shape of the pre-existing enclosure. In order to alleviate this problem, the builders cut into the face of the old rampart, thus creating a little more space for the new houses. They also added a new stone rampart which rose from the base of the earlier ditch and formed the back wall of the new buildings. Within this expanded enclosure, still only around 30m across, a pathway was laid out which ran directly from the enclosure entrance to the doorway of the broch tower. As it reached the doorway, the path split in two to run below the walls on either side of the broch tower. Access in both directions was controlled by

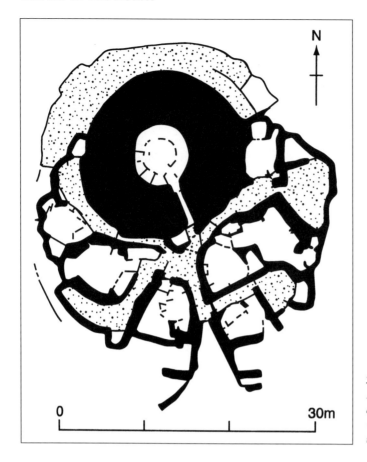

38 *The broch village at Howe. The shaded areas are yards and access routes. Unshaded areas are the remains of roofed buildings*

means of wooden gates, beyond which there were six houses, three on either side of the broch tower. Due to the constraints of the available space, these houses varied slightly in shape but each was fitted out with a nearly identical set of stone furniture: a hearth, an oven, a stone-lined tank, and two cells or cupboards set apart from the main room by flagstone screens. At least one of the houses, and perhaps all of them, had a well-built earth closet or commode, surmounted by a flagstone with an appropriately sized hole.

Each house had access to a small open yard, with small roofed cells leading off, perhaps for the storage of tools or animal feed. These yards were most likely to have been used to shelter domestic animals. Environmental analysis detected the presence of faecal material from a milk-fed calf, and it may be that young or vulnerable animals were housed within the village yards at certain times. It is also possible that the small number of pigs kept by the inhabitants were confined to the village, scavenging scraps of domestic waste, rather than being let loose on the fields where they might have caused considerable damage. Domestic fowl, too, probably ranged around the village. The yards, however, are small, and it seems improbable that they would ever have housed the larger numbers of cattle and sheep upon which the community depended.

The analysis of craft and industrial debris from the site suggests that the houses and yards were kept fairly clean and there is little evidence for activities such as stone- or bone-working. This suggests that only a limited range of domestic activities was carried out within the cramped confines of the village while much of the routine work of daily life went on outside. Although the excavations were more or less confined to the area enclosed by the rampart and ditch, exploratory trenches beyond the enclosure did pick up traces of external buildings. It may be, therefore, that the settlement was rather larger than it now appears, or that ancillary structures, sheds and other outbuildings, lay outside the enclosure.

The building style of the village houses is far removed from that of the Atlantic roundhouse tradition. The houses are small and irregularly shaped with slightly built walls. They would have required only short timbers for roofing and may not have risen more than a few metres above ground level, since they seem to have been confined to a single storey. They huddle together, providing shelter and insulation, and in many ways resemble the traditional Late Bronze Age cellular buildings known from the Northern Isles (chapter 2). Despite these radical architectural changes within the external settlement, however, the spatial arrangements within the broch tower seem similar to what had gone before (**39**), with none of the standardisation of fixtures and fittings seen in the surrounding houses. It has no oven and no stone-lined tank, suggesting that, whatever its function in this period, it was more than just another house within the village.

Who were the villagers?

Clearly each of these six buildings was designed to function as an independent unit, and their small size suggests that each may have housed a group equivalent in size to a nuclear family. If we assume that each building, including the broch tower, did indeed house a nuclear family, and that such families might have averaged approximately seven individuals, then the overall population within the village may have been somewhere around 50. There is a puzzling mismatch between the extraordinarily close proximity within which these people lived and the repetition of the standard set of household fittings from house to house. Given the presence in each house of a hearth, oven and cupboards, it would seem that each household cooked, ate and stored at least some of their food and possessions independently. The multiplicity of yards also suggests that they may have had separate ownership of individual animals. Yet daily life must have involved constant co-operation and negotiation.

So what was the relationship between the members of this community? Perhaps the most immediately attractive model is that the broch village represents a hierarchical settlement with the most powerful family living within the broch tower, surrounded by dependent families of broadly equal status in the surrounding buildings. The relatively high quality of all the houses and their

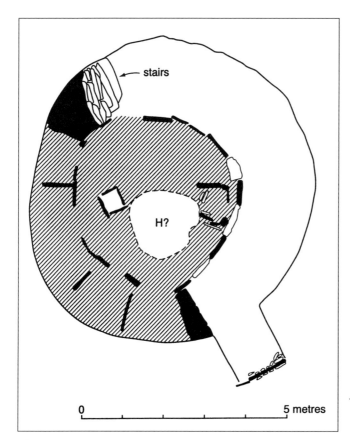

39 *During the broch village period at Howe the spatial arrangements within the tower seem to reflect the traditional layout. A hearth dominated the central area, from which several small cubicles could be accessed. A long paved room formed the northern arc of the interior (the unshaded areas are paved)*

proximity to the broch tower might suggest that these dependent families were themselves of high status, perhaps closely related to the dominant family within a kinship-based social system. So we might see the village community as a locally dominant clan, perhaps claiming descent from the original founders of the settlement, within which the pre-eminent family held sway from the comfort and security of the broch tower.

There are of course other possibilities. It is feasible, for example, that rather than being the dominant house within the village, the broch tower may have been a communal building. It may, for example, have provided storage space for crops and other produce held in common by the community, perhaps also serving as a place to meet, talk, and hold feasts and celebrations. Rather than being a symbol of power for a dominant individual or family, it may instead have been a manifestation of group identity. Or it may have been set aside for a specific group within the community. We are used to thinking in terms of family-based households, but the ethnographic record supplies numerous other models: men and women might have occupied separate dwellings; elders or unmarried adults of either sex might have lived apart from other family-based groups; wealthy men might have had several wives and dependent families spread between one or more houses. Numerous permutations are possible, yet the size and replication of the houses at Howe does lend itself to the more conventional interpretation of closely related but independent, family-based households.

Gurness

Although Howe is the best understood site of its kind, the classic broch village in terms of its scale and organisation remains the site of Gurness, set on an eroding coastline in mainland Orkney (**40** & **colour plate 22**). From 1930–39, Gurness was the subject of a major campaign of excavation which revealed an exceptionally complex collection of buildings associated with a well-preserved broch tower, set within an unusually strong enclosure formed by multiple ramparts and ditches. The excavations, however, were carried out in less than ideal conditions. The first director, Hewat Craw, died suddenly after only four seasons of work, and the excavations were subsequently completed under the nominal direction of J.S. Richardson who, as an Inspector of Ancient Monuments based in Edinburgh, could pay only occasional visits to

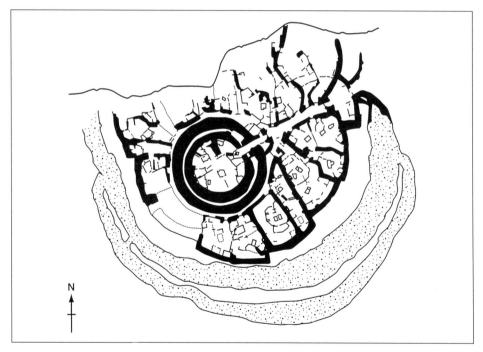

40 *The broch village at Gurness in mainland Orkney is the largest and most obviously planned of these settlements. A complex series of defences, comprising up to three ditches, may once have formed a complete circuit around the village, some parts now being lost to the sea. The innermost of these ramparts is a later addition, comprising a stone wall rising sheer from the base of the inner ditch. The earlier ditch system, however, may pre-date the broch village*

the site. With the intervention of the war, the site was abandoned until the mid-1950s, when it was consolidated for public display, and the excavations were never properly published.

Indeed, it was not until 1987 that a publication was produced by John Hedges, the excavator of Bu, drawing together such limited information as did survive. Hedges' work, however, was largely a study of the surviving architectural features, since the excavators had recorded very little useful information on the nature of the deposits within the buildings. Recording of finds was also erratic. Although nearly 1,000 items of bone, stone and metal were recovered, as well as around 10,000 sherds of pottery, it is virtually impossible to determine how any of this material related to the sequence of occupation. The recording of environmental material was even worse, with only a small sample of the bone assemblage, for example, being retained. Although it appears that cattle, sheep and pigs were exploited by the inhabitants of Gurness, there is no way to compare the overall economy of the site with others excavated under modern conditions. Nonetheless, Gurness remains crucial to any understanding of the Atlantic Scottish Iron Age.

The tower

The broch tower of Gurness is an unusual structure, especially in an Orcadian context. Whereas most Orcadian Atlantic roundhouses are solid-based, Gurness had a continuous ground-level gallery. Unlike the ground-galleried broch towers of western Scotland, however, this seems to have been provided with no means of access from the inner court of the building, and could only be entered through narrow creeps in each of the two guard cells at the entrance. The intra-mural stair which would have given access to the upper floors started at the level above the ground-floor gallery and was entered through a door nearly 2m above the internal floor. This was presumably accessed by means of a ladder or wooden stair.

The lack of easy access suggests that the builders intended the ground-floor gallery to have a purely structural function, perhaps to reduce the overall volume of stone required in the building. Whatever purpose the builders had in mind, however, the ground-floor gallery seems to have quickly become a dangerous liability. Dramatic slumping visible in elements of the walling shows that what must have been an immensely heavy superstructure began to exert extreme stresses on the lower walls of the building, especially over door frames and other weak points. As a result, the occupants deliberately and methodically filled up the ground-floor gallery with tightly packed stone rubble, creating what was, in effect, a solid-based building. This must have been an extraordinarily difficult, dangerous and cumbersome process given that each stone had to be painstakingly manoeuvred through the cramped access to this gallery and then manhandled around to the required point in the circuit under perhaps 2,000 tons of decidedly unstable masonry.

Although laid out in much the same way, using slab partitions to define small rooms and compartments, the surviving internal plan of the Gurness broch tower is rather different from those at Bu and Howe (**41** & **colour plate 17**). Essentially, the interior seems to have been divided into two separate houses. Anyone entering was first required to negotiate the entrance passage, where flagstone door jambs, a pivot stone and two opposed bar-holes testified to the former presence of a stout and secure wooden door, behind which were two 'guard-cells'. Once through the passage, there was no choice but to turn right into a roughly triangular room equipped with a substantial two-storey cupboard or dresser, built from flagstones. This then gave access to a narrow corridor with further 'double-decker' cupboards at either end. Once in this corridor, there was a choice between entering one of two chambers, each of which seem to represent a separate domestic focus within the building, or a third smaller room which lacked any sign of a hearth.

The southern and larger chamber was semi-circular, the arc of its south wall being formed by the inner face of the broch tower itself. This room was dominated by a large hearth, carefully paved and kerbed on three sides. At either end were further double-decker cupboards or compartments. The purpose of these compartments is not immediately obvious, but it seems quite

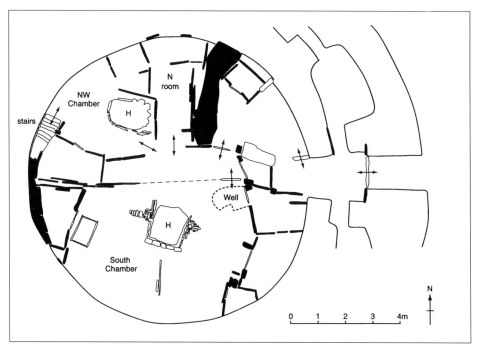

41 *Simplified plan showing the internal arrangement of space within the broch tower at Gurness. This plan reflects the final coherent layout, still visible on the site today. It most probably dates to the late first or second century AD, by which time the broch tower may have been significantly reduced in height. The disturbed and partial remains of earlier floors still survive below the internal furniture*

likely that at least some of them were the equivalent of 'box-beds' which could have been lined with organic material such as straw or bracken, and hung with hides or textiles to make comfortable sleeping areas.

Across the corridor from the southern chamber was a smaller room occupying the north-west of the broch interior. Again there was a hearth, and double-decker compartments. This room also contained other features not present in the southern chamber, including a well-built cupboard or 'aumbry' recessed into the original wall of the broch tower at around head height. Most importantly, however, it contained a steep flight of 14 steps rising against the wall of the broch tower. This stair was clearly not an original component of the broch tower since it obscured part of the original scarcement and was not bonded into the broch masonry. It was, however, an integral component of the various chamber walls and double-decker cupboards which converge at this point in the interior (41), thus demonstrating that these features too were not primary constructions.

In general the early excavators stopped digging when they reached these solidly-built flagstone features and associated paving, since one of the main goals of the excavation was to lay out the impressive architecture of the site for public display. In some places, however, they did lift the paving and carry out limited areas of excavation below this level. This limited work was enough to confirm that the layout of rooms described above is not absolutely primary to the building of the broch tower. For example, below the central corridor the excavators found the buried remains of a central hearth, suggesting the interior may originally have been laid out as a single large house, like those at Bu and Howe. They also discovered the entrance to a large stone well, reached via a steep flight of stone steps, which had been covered over by the later paving; an enigmatic structure to which we will return later.

The village

Surrounding the broch tower is a village of tightly clustered houses covering more than 1,000m². All were accessed by a narrow paved passage, like that at Howe, which runs from the gatehouse straight towards the entrance to the broch tower. At the broch entrance, the path divides to run around the base of the tower: both branches were barred, again as at Howe, by wooden gates. Each of the buildings within the village was rather different in size and design, ranging from 14-75m², although they shared many features in common. Most were subdivided into two or more internal 'houses' each with their own hearth and furniture, and usually with independent access to the main passage. Some of these internal subdivisions may have been put in place long after the original laying out of the houses, but the rudimentary nature of the excavation records makes it impossible to be sure in most cases. Almost all of the houses contained well-built stone furniture including box-beds, cupboards, ovens, tanks and earth closets very similar to those at Howe. What was apparently missing, at least when compared to Howe, was provision of open space. Indeed virtually the whole of the enclosed area would have been a sea of roofs, with the only open space being the narrow access passage (unless of course it too was roofed).

Quite how these roofs were constructed is an issue that has never been satisfactorily addressed. They seem to have rested on rubble walls less than 1m thick, each shared between two adjoining buildings. Although the force of the rafters pushing downwards from both directions may have held these narrow common walls in place, they still seem remarkably slight to have supported the required weight of timber and thatch. Quite how the thatch would have shed water in such a tightly-packed conglomeration of buildings is another question that has never been properly answered. There must clearly have been considerable sophistication of roofing and drainage mechanisms in place to prevent the village turning rapidly into a swamp. The lack of provision for yards also suggests that life was lived somewhat differently in the Gurness village than at Howe. Although there may have been some provision for housing a few young or sick animals within the village, most activities relating to husbandry must surely have been conducted outside the confines of the enclosure.

The development of the broch village

When Hewat Craw first set out his interpretation of the settlement sequence at Gurness during the early stages of the excavation programme, he believed that the broch tower had originally stood alone within its defensive ditches (**42**). At a later stage, he thought, once the structure had outlived its original

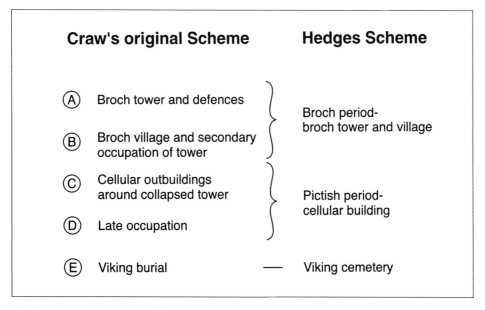

42 *The original interpretation of the Gurness sequence by the first excavator, Hewat Craw, has been revised by John Hedges*

defensive purpose, the broch village was constructed around it and additional houses were built within the shell of the broch tower, creating the picture that we see laid out on the site today. Although he subsequently modified his views a little (deciding that the features inside the tower were probably of more or less the same kind as those that were present originally), it was his initial statement of the sequence which was to become the conventional view.

This view has since been questioned, however, most influentially by John Hedges in his definitive publication of the site (**42**). The conventional view, he argued, was based on the assumption that broch towers were essentially defensive refuges rather than settlements, leading to the belief that their original layout should be unencumbered by the clutter of domestic occupation seen at Gurness. In other words, it was expectation rather than evidence which had led to the internal features and the surrounding village being dismissed as later, squatter occupation. Hedges believed that there was in fact no evidence to suggest that the internal stone structures and the associated village were anything other than contemporary with the broch tower. He believed that the whole complex had been conceived as a single building operation and that, despite considerable modification and rebuilding both within and around the broch tower at various points in the site's history, the village as it appears today is essentially what was intended from the start.

Other archaeologists have disagreed with Hedges' reinterpretation. The most prominent among these has been Euan MacKie, who has pointed out several clear instances where internal structures within the broch tower cannot have been contemporary with its original construction. For example, the stone staircase inside the tower rises up over the scarcement, which, in MacKie's view, ought to have formed a continuous circuit supporting a wooden floor. There is also good evidence that some of the architectural features now present within the tower were constructed when its height had already been considerably reduced. Unfortunately, while MacKie's arguments for the stratigraphic depth of the architectural features are certainly valid, this does not really get us much closer to resolving the basic argument. Simply because some of the visible features are secondary does not mean that the original layout was significantly different in character. Certainly at Howe, the most closely analogous site, the successive roundhouses each had remarkably similar internal arrangements. The striking similarities between Gurness and Howe would tend to suggest, in the absence of evidence to the contrary, that the sequence at the two sites might have followed a similar pattern. In other words, there may very well have been a long sequence of Atlantic round-houses at Gurness, of which the surviving broch tower is simply the final version. The associated village may have been primary, or it may have been added later: given the large size of the space enclosed by the surrounding ditches, it seems quite possible that a substantial settlement was envisaged from the start.

Village life

Judging by the number of individual houses and hearths, and allowing for the area lost to coastal erosion, John Hedges has estimated that the Gurness village may have housed between 200 and 400 people at its height. This would have been an immensely large congregation of people in a region where the most common settlement pattern throughout prehistory had comprised scattered farmsteads, usually of one or two houses at most. Indeed, there are many factors about the Gurness broch village which suggest that it would have been an extraordinary place to have visited.

Walking around the ruins of the village today, the site seems open and bright. When occupied, however, it would have assaulted the senses from all sides. Visiting Gurness during the Iron Age would have been a daunting experience, as was clearly intended by its builders. From a distance, by land or sea, it would have caught the eye as a sprawling mass of thatched roofs spewing smoke, clustered around the brooding mass of the central tower. The dead zone of the outer ditches and ramparts, and the sheer stone face of the inner rampart would have restricted access to the single narrow causeway straddled by the stone gatehouse. There all visitors could be inspected, admitted, rejected, or just kept waiting. Assuming that access was permitted, the visitor would then emerge through the rear door of the gatehouse, into the village itself. The narrow path, dark, claustrophobic and smelly, would have pointed the visitor one way only: straight towards the barred door of the broch tower. There was no horizon, no view beyond the stone house walls which pressed in on either side and the looming bulk of the broch tower, to which the eye was inexorably drawn, rising above the far end of the passage. Walking along the path, passing barred wooden doors and under the drip of wet thatch, a further series of obstacles remained to be negotiated; the outer chamber attached to the front of the broch tower provided another point where visitors could be vetted or intimidated, then another stop at the door midway along the broch entrance passage, before final admission into the heart of the tower.

For the inhabitants, too, this would have been a remarkable place, revolutionary perhaps for people whose parents and grandparents most probably farmed independently from scattered farmsteads in the surrounding countryside. This was a closed community. You either lived within the walls or you did not. There was no middle ground. It was a place where people's movements and actions could be watched and controlled, and where social norms would be hard to break. Only one path led in or out; the houses shared common walls, and were often simply subdivisions within a larger building. Entering or leaving the village would have taken on a processional quality, passing the doors of neighbours, squeezing past others on their way home or out into the fields. This was not a place to keep secrets. The comings and goings of each inhabitant and family group would have been obvious to all. It was a sheltered, covered, protected environment, but one where common values, communal lifestyles and co-operative ventures would have been hard to challenge.

Architecture is not simply a passive reflection of social structure, but also serves to reinforce certain values and social principles. For example, although the broch village at Gurness may have been laid out to reflect the social dominance of a single family within a wider kinship group, once built, it would have formed a remarkably potent symbol of social authority in its own right. For subsequent generations, growing up within the maze of passages and interconnected houses around the broch tower, their daily routines and their perception of the 'natural order' of society would have been shaped and constrained by the architecture itself. The separateness, difference and dominance of the broch tower within a tight-knit cluster of otherwise stan- dardised buildings, would have reinforced the social dominance of those within. The seclusion of the village itself, an island within its deep ditch and broad rampart, would have set the village community apart from outsiders. Once built, the broch village did not simply reflect the social life and world view of its inhabitants; it silently but surely moulded and refined them.

Broch villages of Orkney and Caithness

No other site approaches Gurness in terms of its scale and cohesion, but enough broch villages are now known in Orkney to suggest that this became a common settlement form in the last centuries BC. Indeed, Hedges has estimated that around 20 may be identified from field survey and the records of antiquarian excavation. The broch village of Midhowe lies on the coast of Rousay, facing Gurness across the narrow sound. It too was excavated during the pre-war period and laid out as a public monument. In size and layout the village appears more like Howe than Gurness, as the handful of houses have been accommodated within the cramped confines of the peninsula on which it lies. The architecture of the broch tower, however, is so like that at Gurness that Euan MacKie has suggested that it may have been built by the same architect. The only site to approach Gurness in terms of its size and complexity, however, is the broch village of Lingro, known only from fairly rudimentary antiquarian excavations (**43**).

Outside Orkney, broch villages are sparse. Only in Caithness are there sites which appear similar to the Orcadian examples, the settlement at Keiss Road being one notable example. There are no signs, however, of any similar sites in other parts of Atlantic Scotland. In Shetland, despite the agglomeration of outbuildings around some Atlantic roundhouses, there is no sign of the scale or spatial order of settlement associated with sites like Gurness and Lingro. The sprawling layout of the Iron Age settlement at Jarlshof, for example, was formed by the periodic replacement of successive structures. Similarly,

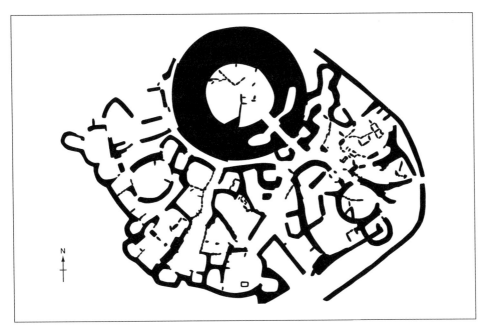

43 *The site of Lingro is known only from the fragmentary records of antiquarian excavation and is now largely destroyed. From the plan, however, it appears to have been a major broch village, the largest and most complex known after Gurness*

although some of the finest examples of broch architecture occur in the west, notably at Dun Carloway, Dun Troddan and Dun Telve, these stand alone with no more than a scatter of outbuildings. Whatever social changes promoted the creation of these new and highly structured centres of population in Orkney, they clearly did not have the same effect further north or west.

Dating the broch villages

It is unfortunate that the dating evidence associated with the broch villages at both Howe and Gurness is fairly limited. In both cases, the period during which they were occupied lasted for several centuries: we can be sure that both were thriving during the first century AD, but their origins are more obscure. The earliest radiocarbon dates from the broch village phase at Howe reflect a period when the original buildings had already been destroyed by fire, perhaps during the first century BC. Later, in the first century AD, in the wake of various rebuilds and localised structural collapse, the settlement began to lose its definition and the well-defined village layout began to lose its focus. The broch tower itself seems to have substantially collapsed during this period, to the extent that the intra-mural stair was left open to the elements. Nonetheless the settlement remained in use until at least the fourth century AD.

The features visible today inside the broch tower at Gurness can be dated to no earlier than the later part of the first century AD, on the basis of a small glass bead and toggle, probably made from melted-down Roman glass, which were found below the final floor. Indeed, the village as we now see it was almost certainly a product of the first two centuries AD, when the community at Gurness was well-established, successful and expanding in numbers. This need not, however, be the whole story. Finds of saddle querns, which seem to have been replaced by the more efficient rotary quern some time around 200 BC, suggest that the earliest occupation within the tower may have been substantially earlier. The stratigraphic evidence is very poor, but it was certainly the view of the original excavator that saddle querns were associated with the earlier levels, and rotary querns with the later. This claim cannot be substantiated from the impoverished documentation which survives from the excavations, and it was dismissed by John Hedges who believed that the broch tower was a construction of the Roman period. Nonetheless, Craw's claim was based on first-hand observation and the presence of earlier activity would be consistent with the situation at Howe. There is, in fact, nothing to suggest that the broch tower at Gurness does not overlie a similar sequence of earlier roundhouses to that found at Howe. Whatever the date of its foundation, the settlement at Gurness, like Howe, survived well into the first millennium AD, evolving into a nucleated village of the Pictish period.

Wells, shrines and the power of the ancestors

Although it seems clear that the architecture of broch villages both reflected and promoted the power of prominent individuals or families, this does not necessarily mean that they were simply prehistoric versions of the medieval castle and its keep. These later buildings were manifestations of secular power, quite distinct from the religious authority represented by the church. In the Iron Age, as we saw in chapter 4, such distinctions between the secular and the sacred did not apply to anything like the same extent.

The description of Gurness given above made passing mention of the well, set within the primary floor, but it is becoming increasingly clear that this extraordinary structure may have been more than simply a convenient water source. The Gurness well was most likely built at the same time as the broch tower itself, if not earlier. The construction process involved more than the straightforward digging of a shaft (**44**). It began with the excavation of a huge hole in the underlying rock, some 5.5m across and around 4m deep. Within this cavity was then built an elaborate drystone construction very much in the broch architectural style, incorporating stairs, hollow chambers and corbelled cells. Access involved a short drop from the broch floor onto a small landing from which a precipitous descent could be made down a flight of 18 stone

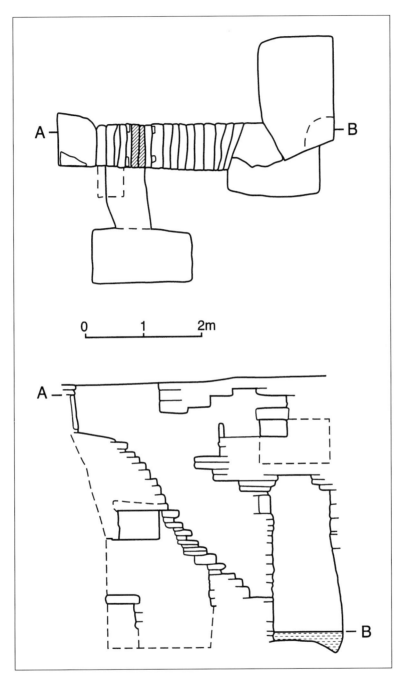

0 1 2m

44 *This diagrammatic view gives some impression of the structural complexity of the 'well' in the early broch tower floor at Gurness. It is far more elaborate than would be required simply to retrieve water*

steps. At the bottom was a slight vertical drop of less than a metre into a small cistern, where a shallow pool of water would have formed. The roof of the well was an elaborate corbelled construction, and various small corbelled cells were incorporated both within the roof and below the steps. From the interior of the broch tower, however, all that was visible was a small access shaft.

As occupation continued above, the structural components of the well began to settle and the whole central area of the overlying floor appears to have slumped. This alarming development seems to have necessitated periodic levelling-up of the floor of the broch tower and eventually the entrance to the well was paved over and sealed.

The sophistication of design of the Gurness well is in marked contrast to its impracticality as a water source. Indeed, the structure defies any purely functional explanation. It seems highly unlikely that anyone would wish routinely to negotiate 18 steep, slippery steps whilst laden with buckets of water: a simple shaft down which a bucket could be dropped would have served the purpose just as well. Given the small capacity of the cistern, it seems unlikely that the well could ever have provided a sufficient water supply for the inhabitants of the broch village. Instead, the importance of the well may lie in its ritual or religious significance.

Wells, shafts and pits are often associated in later prehistoric Europe with religious beliefs and practices. Grain storage pits in southern English hillforts like Danebury in Hampshire, for example, were often the focus for offerings to the gods. Sometimes these offerings comprised agricultural produce or animals, but occasionally human bodies or body parts were also placed within the pits. Across the English Channel at much the same time, rituals at the Gallic sanctuary of Gournay-sur-Aronde in Picardy centred on the sacrifice and deposition of bulls within a deep central pit. Closer to home, the Pictish royal fortress of Burghead in Moray seems to have incorporated an elaborate, ritual well in the mid-first millennium AD. More widely in Europe, it has been suggested that Iron Age religion may often have involved the worship of chthonic deities, by means of wells, pits and shafts that gave access to the Otherworld below the earth. It is tempting to see the well at Gurness in this light.

The case is perhaps strengthened by the recent rediscovery of a remarkably similar structure at Mine Howe, also in Orkney. Mine Howe itself is a large mound now known to have been surrounded in the Iron Age by a substantial ditch. From the top of the mound, a series of steps lead down to a landing from which two short lengths of gallery are accessible. From the landing, the steps continue down until they reach a short vertical drop into a cistern or tank at the bottom. There may have been other buildings on the top or sides of the mound, but the well was clearly the centrepiece of the monument. The site seems to have attracted considerable activity, and the ongoing excavations have found objects of Iron Age, Roman and Pictish date. Indeed, Mine Howe was evidently a place of considerable religious significance, perhaps a shrine or oracle, which attracted people over several centuries. While it was not directly associated with any form of Atlantic roundhouse (although there is probably at least one nearby), Mine Howe has clear implications for our interpretation of the well at Gurness, and thus for the status and function of the broch tower within which it was enclosed.

Although the Gurness example is the best known and most elaborate, wells have been recorded within many Orcadian Atlantic roundhouses. Even where wells do not occur, as at Howe, other subterranean structures may have served a similar purpose. The chamber of the Neolithic tomb at Howe, on which the successive roundhouses were built, was extended and maintained as an 'earth-house' beneath the floors of the later buildings. The tomb's entrance passage was also extended and modified to act as a drain and water tank associated with the first roundhouse on the site. When this drain went out of use, the remains of two individuals, a teenage boy and a young woman, were placed within it. This not only suggests that the tomb retained some religious significance for the Iron Age inhabitants; it also raises the possibility that it may have been the presence of the ancient tomb that attracted the round-house-builders in the first place.

Another Orcadian roundhouse, at Quanterness, was also built adjacent to a chambered tomb and again reused the former burial chamber as an 'earth-house' or souterrain. Other Atlantic roundhouses are almost certainly built over the remains of earlier tombs, although this is more or less impossible to prove without excavation. Although practicality might suggest that the ruined tombs were seen as little more than a handy source of building stone, the specific ways in which they were reused at Howe and Quanterness, together with the ritualistic aspects of Iron Age domestic life in general, suggests that they may have retained a deeper significance.

Farmstead to castle?

Studies of the ethnographic record suggest that there are very few non-state societies in which warfare and violence do not figure to some degree, and the Iron Age communities of Atlantic Scotland were probably no exception. The nature of warfare in such societies, however, can vary enormously. During the Atlantic Scottish Iron Age, it is likely that society at a local level was organised in kinship-based groups, into what we might loosely call tribes or clans. There may also have been higher authorities of some kind, as we shall discuss below. Such communities probably engaged in conflict at various levels. Feuding between neighbouring kin-groups, perhaps over rights to land and resources, would probably have been an ever present part of life, and on occasion no doubt spilled over into violent conflict. There is little to suggest, however, that these communities were particularly well-armed, and little evidence for any sort of military 'culture' or warrior ideology. Warfare was most likely small-scale and sporadic. In such a context, there would have been few, if any, large-scale battles. Even less likely is the sort of siege warfare conjured up by traditional images of the broch towers as defensive refuges.

The situation may have changed, however, towards the end of the first millennium BC. The expansion of the Roman Empire far to the south, particularly during the last century BC when Caesar completed the conquest of Gaul, had far-reaching effects on communities well beyond its boundaries. Much of the Roman economy was driven by slave labour, and an important by-product of military campaigning was the provision of slaves to work on estate farms in Italy and elsewhere. Even before the conquest, Mediterranean luxury goods (especially wine) had been exported to Gaul in considerable quantities. Gaulish tribal élites were keen to enhance their own prestige by gaining access to Roman luxury goods. Among the 'products' that flowed in the opposite direction were slaves. Indeed the Roman demand for slave labour may have been ultimately responsible for the destabilisation of the native economy in many parts of Gaul. The virtual emptying of the countryside as communities moved from open rural settlements to heavily enclosed hillforts during the first century BC may be a result of this process.

As Roman interests expanded into southern Britain, these same processes would have affected British Iron Age societies. This may have begun as early as the mid-first century BC, several generations before the Claudian conquest, as southern British tribes were closely involved in the political and military machinations associated with Caesar's conquest of Gaul. Although Caesar's invasion of southern England did not result in conquest, the southern tribes were now firmly part of the sphere of Roman interest. It is entirely possible that organised or speculative raids around the coasts of Britain could have affected communities as far north as Atlantic Scotland.

Warfare is not always easy to identify archaeologically. As we have seen, many Atlantic roundhouses were probably fairly low-walled, with thatched timber roofs resting on a wall-head at first- or second-floor level. These would have been no more or less defensively secure than their timber counterparts in the south and east of Scotland. The earliest roundhouses, such as Bu, were apparently of this type; stout-walled but essentially undefended farmhouses. Some of the more sophisticated, taller broch towers, however, contain features which many archaeologists have interpreted as defensive, and broch villages tended to be enclosed within ramparts and ditches. Superficially at least, this might suggest that there was more concern with defence towards the end of the first millennium BC.

The traditional interpretation of broch towers as defensive strongholds is hardly surprising, given their superficial resemblance to later castles and tower-houses. This interpretation, however, is hard to sustain in detail. In fact, the defensive capacities of even the tallest broch towers were probably fairly limited, especially when compared with some of the hillforts found elsewhere in Iron Age Scotland. Although the featureless stone shell of the broch tower with its low, narrow entrance would have made it difficult for prospective attackers to force access, it would have been equally difficult for the inhabitants to do much in the way of active defence. Many older reconstruction drawings of brochs show defenders using the wall-head as a fighting platform from which to repel attackers, in the much the same way as the battlements of medieval castles were later used. Since Mousa is the only broch tower with an obvious route of access to the wall-head, however, this was probably not a common practice. Several broch towers have gaps between the lintels of their entrance passages through which, it is argued, defenders could have poked their spears to deter any assailants attacking the door below. Otherwise, defending a broch tower may have involved little more than bolting the door and waiting for danger to pass. Any attackers with sufficient time on their hands could presumably have blocked up or set fire to the entrance, smoking or starving the defenders out. Any with a grudge could presumably have laid waste to the surrounding fields and absconded with any animals which the inhabitants had failed to gather into the tower.

In fact, the main defensive qualities of Atlantic roundhouses often derive more from their siting and associated outworks than from the structures themselves. Multiple ramparts and ditches as at Gurness (**colour plate 22**), or thick enclosing walls as at Clickhimin in Shetland (**colour plate 1**), seem to present a more serious barrier to potential attackers than the structures inside them. The same can be said for the numerous islet-sited roundhouses of the Western Isles, where access could have been relatively easily controlled via narrow causeways and blocking walls. Dun Loch an Duna at Bragar in Lewis has three separate cross-walls (not all necessarily contemporary) which control access across the causeway, while an enclosing wall encircles a large area of ground to the rear of the islet, where stock could have been protected (**45**). On sites like these, the presence of the broch tower seems almost incidental to the defensive capacities of the site.

Some of the most architecturally accomplished broch towers, however, seem to have been sited with no thought for any sort of defensive capability. Loch na Beirgh in Lewis, for example, occupies what was once a low-lying islet. The adjacent shore rises steeply to high ground from which potential attackers could easily have rained down fire and missiles on the thatched roof. In Shetland too, Fojut has pointed out that the ability to command extensive views seems to have been an optional extra for the roundhouse-builders. Had defence been a major consideration, it would presumably have been vital to be forewarned of any likely attack. Clearly the perceived need for defence varied from place to place.

A further complicating factor is the difficulty in distinguishing between 'defences' built to serve a practical need, and those intended to demonstrate

45 *Dun Loch an Duna, Bragar, Lewis: the islet on which this complex roundhouse sits is surrounded by an enclosure wall and its narrow causeway is protected by three walls, which may represent successive renewals of the barrier.* Photograph: D.W. Harding

the status and prestige of the inhabitants. This problem has been explored in other parts of Iron Age Britain. In southern England for example, hillforts such as Maiden Castle in Dorset seem to have developed ever larger and more complex systems of banks and ditches, which may suggest an increasingly sophisticated tactical approach to Iron Age warfare. Alternatively, they may reflect the growing desire of the inhabitants to display their prestige through the deployment of labour and resources drawn from neighbouring communities. The building and repair of these ramparts, probably on an annual basis, may have formed a prime means by which the authority centred in the hillfort was maintained. Well-argued cases have been made on both sides of the discussion. The problem is that actual military strength and symbolic military strength may end up looking rather similar to the archaeologist.

This is essentially the same dilemma that faces us in assessing the degree to which heavily enclosed broch villages like Gurness were intended for practical defensive purposes. Certainly the combination of sheer stone wall and outer ditches would have given the defenders the edge had the settlement ever been attacked, yet the role of the defences in creating a closed, self-contained community, set apart from the outside world, may ultimately have been more important.

Brochs and Rome

Mentions of Atlantic Scotland in the classical literature are few and tantalising, and the two most important references give contrasting views of the relationship between the people of Orkney and the Roman Empire. In a work dating to the later fourth century AD, the Roman writer Eutropius records that the Orkney Islands submitted to the Emperor Claudius during his invasion of southern England in AD 43. Some archaeologists have dismissed this as a simple copying mistake by a later scribe, or perhaps a misunderstanding on the part of Eutropius himself, since it seemed implausible that an Iron Age society in such an apparently remote area should have had such an acute and timely awareness of the appropriate diplomatic niceties. More recently, however, Andrew Fitzpatrick has linked Eutropius' statement with the recovery of two sherds of pottery from the 1930s excavations at Gurness. These sherds, one from the broch tower and one from the outbuildings (but possibly originating from the same pot) belong to a smashed Roman wine amphora of type known to archaeologists as Haltern 70. This type of vessel was used essentially as a transport container for trade goods and is known to have carried both liqueur wine and ripe olives preserved in wine.

The finding of a Roman amphora in Orkney would have been remarkable enough, but this particular find is even more surprising since Haltern 70 amphorae were produced only until around AD 60. This would appear to date the Gurness amphora at least 20 years before Agricola's invasion of Scotland. So how can we explain its occurrence in the far north, nearly 1,000km from the nearest comparable example?

Although amphorae of this date and type are otherwise unknown in Scotland, they do occur in south-east England at sites like Bagendon and St Albans, which were centres of powerful tribal élites before and during the Roman invasion. These élites appear to have adopted many aspects of Roman culture well before the Claudian invasion. Indeed, John Creighton has recently suggested that many of their leaders may even have been brought up and educated in Rome, as hostages or 'obsides', a common practice in many parts of the Empire at this time. Many such individuals would certainly have pledged their allegiance to Claudius in AD 43, at the time of the supposed Orcadian submission. Fitzpatrick has proposed that both the Gurness amphora and the Orcadian submission to Claudius may reflect close ties of alliance or kinship between the élites of Orkney and their Romanised contemporaries in south-east England. In this scenario, the Gurness amphora may have been dispatched to the north as part of the gift exchanges associated with marriage celebrations, or the making and sealing of alliances. Although impossible to prove, this is an attractive hypothesis and the only one so far proposed to explain the Gurness find.

The second documented encounter between the communities of Orkney and the Roman Empire was rather more confrontational. The reference in question comes from Tacitus writing in the early first century AD about the career of his father-in-law, Agricola. Tacitus records that, following his decisive defeat of the Caledonian tribes at Mons Graupius, Agricola's navy circumnavigated Scotland carrying out devastating raids on Orkney and elsewhere. The implication is that Orcadian forces had formed part of the defeated Caledonian army. By the early AD 80s, therefore, any arrangements made with Rome had apparently long since lapsed.

Beyond these fragments, Roman references to Atlantic Scotland are virtually non-existent, and we must turn instead to the archaeological evidence. This too is scant: compared to other areas on the periphery of the Empire, Atlantic Scottish sites have yielded few Roman objects. Most Roman material in the region dates to the late first and second centuries AD, from the period of Agricola's invasion and partial conquest to the construction and abandonment of the Antonine Wall across the Forth-Clyde isthmus.

Roman objects of this period have been found in the secondary levels of numerous Atlantic roundhouses. The broch village of Midhowe, for example, produced fragments of high quality Samian pottery, as well as a fine bronze patera (a round flat dish). Indeed, there seems to have been a distinct preference for the importation of the higher quality products on offer from the Roman world; although Midhowe and a few other sites have produced fragments of more mundane, coarse pottery, Samian ware is found in significantly greater proportions than would be the case on all but the wealthiest Roman sites.

Some of these exotic imports may have remained in use for many years. Two of the Samian sherds from Oxtro in Orkney, for example, show signs of attempted repair, while another had been ground down to be used as a pigment. A few small objects from Gurness and elsewhere were made from melted-down Roman glass, perhaps recycling the remains of once-prized Roman vases or drinking cups. Occasional attempts were even made to imitate Roman objects in steatite and other locally available materials.

Most of the objects imported from the Roman world were designed for use in feasting, drinking, and the entertaining of guests, where the possession and display of exotic objects would have enhanced the prestige of the host. Other objects, common in the Roman world itself, are correspondingly rare in the far north. Roman coinage, for example, is extremely scarce. Indeed, the only Roman coins known from Atlantic roundhouse sites belong to a group of six or seven *denarii* recovered from the broch village of Lingro during the nineteenth century (and subsequently lost). The coins ranged in date from the reign of Vespasian (AD 69-79) until that of Crispina (AD 180-3). Other unusual finds include a pottery model of a bale of fleeces from Dun Fiadhairt in Skye. This may have been a votive offering made by a Roman merchant, and perhaps a rare reflection of trade between Roman and native.

This small, yet diverse, collection of Roman imports is difficult to interpret archaeologically and it is easier to say what it does not represent than what it does. There is little, for example, to suggest sustained or organised trade with the Empire. There is also no indication of any Roman coin hoards like those further south, which are often interpreted as bribes from Rome to ensure good behaviour on the part of the natives. The material which does occur may be the product of occasional trading expeditions by Roman merchants. We know from Tacitus that such individuals were active in Ireland where a similarly disparate collection of material has been found, and there is no reason why Atlantic Scotland may not also have been visited. Some of the objects may have infiltrated native exchange systems, perhaps changing hands several times, as gifts from one individual to another, until they reached their final destination. Others may, however, have originated as booty from military campaigns, the product of scavenging on abandoned sites or as souvenirs carried home by mercenaries, refugees, missionaries or adventurers.

Kings of Orkney?

There does seem to have been a marked social change in Orkney during the course of the Iron Age. The early part of the period was characterised by dispersed farming communities occupying relatively modest Atlantic roundhouses, like those at Bu or Quanterness. These first roundhouse-builders were apparently fairly prosperous and had a fair degree of local autonomy, but there is little suggest to that they were members of a social élite. By the end of the millennium, however, this had changed, and broch villages like Gurness, Lingro, Howe and Midhowe show the existence of a more hierarchical society, in which groups of people were gathered together in substantially larger settlements. While the first Atlantic roundhouses may be seen as symbols of control over land, broch villages were symbols of control over people.

The degree to which power was concentrated in Orkney during the first century BC is debatable. At one end of the scale of possibilities, it may be that Gurness, as the largest and most complex broch village, had royal status, housing a family whose political power extended throughout Orkney. Indeed their influence may have extended much further, through alliances of kinship and marriage with tribal rulers far to the south. How else might we explain how the inhabitants of Gurness acquired access to imported Mediterranean wine and olives more than a generation before the Roman army first campaigned in Scotland? Indeed, one could speculate that the development of élite centres in Orkney based around the broch villages, coupled with their failure to take root in other areas like Shetland and the Western Isles, might even reflect Orcadian hegemony over a much wider area. Alternatively, Gurness may have housed a terrified clan, one of many in Orkney, huddled together for protection from southern slave raiders. The reality probably lies somewhere in between.

6

TOWERS IN THE SOUTH?

Although the overwhelming majority of Atlantic roundhouses are found in northern and western Scotland, there are similar monuments in some parts of the south and east (**46**). Since later land use in these areas has generally been more destructive than in the Highlands and Islands, however, none of these 'southern brochs' are particularly well-preserved. Although several contain intra-mural cells, stairs and guard cells, only Torwood near Stirling survives to a sufficient height to confirm the presence of a scarcement ledge. It is far from clear, therefore, whether any of the southern brochs ever reached the tower-like proportions of the most sophisticated northern examples.

The existence of these southern brochs has always been something of a puzzle. How did they come to be built so far from the main concentrations, and why do intervening areas, such as the north-east of Scotland, contain no obvious parallels? The answer has often been to see the southern brochs as the products of northern intruders, and they have thus tended to be interpreted as exotic and alien to the regions in which they are found. As we shall see, however, this approach may be a little misleading.

A tale of two brochs

The main concentration of southern brochs lies in the Upper Forth Valley, close to Stirling. Over the last few centuries aggressive land reclamation has reduced the once extensive wetlands of this landscape to a few remnant bogs. In prehistory, however, this was treacherous marshland and permanent occupation was largely restricted to the hillsides overlooking the floodplain. Land passage from north to south was limited to a few constricted routes of which the most important was that later controlled by Stirling Castle.

Leckie
The site of Leckie occupies an inland promontory overlooking the valley. Its location on rising ground would have given its inhabitants access to the

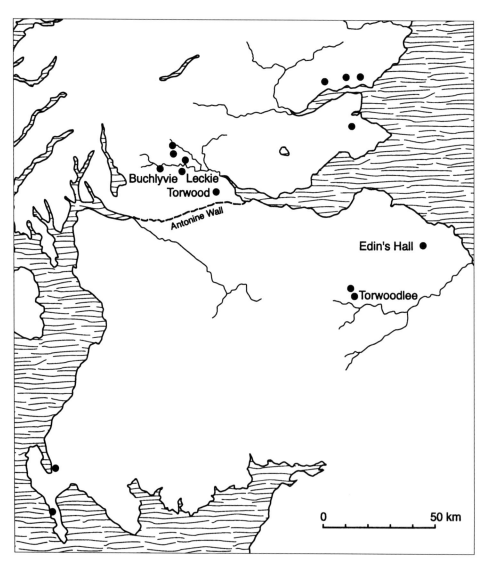

Buchlyvie Leckie
Torwood ●

Antonine Wall

Edin's Hall ●

●Torwoodlee

0   50 km

46 *The distribution of known southern brochs divides into four groups: one cluster in the Upper Forth Valley; another around the Firth of Tay; a scatter in the south-east uplands; and two in the far south-west. Other areas contain numerous unexcavated stone-walled roundhouses variously referred to as duns or homesteads, and many of these ruins may well conceal intra-mural architectural features (the excavated site at Buchlyvie, for example, was a featureless mound prior to excavation). This map should thus be seen as a rather minimal representation of the likely distribution of these sites. The map also shows the location of the Antonine Wall built in the mid-second century AD*

cultivable land of the valley sides and the rough pasture of the Gargunnock Hills to the south, as well as the natural wetland resources of the valley floor. The site was excavated by Euan MacKie during the 1970s and, despite the modest survival of the superstructure, the floor deposits produced a wealth of information.

Even before the broch was built, there seems to have been some occupation at Leckie. A group of post-holes and a hearth indicate the existence of an earlier house, probably dating to the first century BC. This building was later replaced by the broch, but it is not clear whether there was any intervening period of abandonment. The broch itself was irregularly shaped, almost square in outline, and survived only to a height of around 1.5m (**47**). Its walls contained a single intra-mural cell which gave access to a flight of stairs. The eccentric plan of the building reflects the surface irregularities of the site and it seems unlikely that it ever boasted a tower-like superstructure, despite having stone walls nearly 6m thick in places. The interior of the broch was dominated by a large central hearth, suggesting that the ground floor formed the main living space. A ring of substantial post-holes, concentric with the inner wall-face, probably supported either the roof or an upper floor.

A number of sherds of fine Samian pottery show that the site's inhabitants maintained close contacts with the Roman world, perhaps even before the building of the broch (since some of the sherds are apparently associated with the pre-broch structure). These vessels would have been obtained during the Flavian period, in the late first century AD. This was the period of Agricola's conquest and short-lived occupation of southern and eastern Scotland, during which Roman influence extended some distance north of the Forth Valley. Sherds of later pottery show renewed Roman contacts during the Antonine period, in the mid-second century AD, when Leckie lay a short distance north of the Antonine Wall (**46**).

The subsequent abandonment of Leckie was accompanied by the violent destruction of the building. Many of the stones within the walls had been severely cracked and scorched by the intense heat, while the upper parts of the walls had seemingly been cast down into the fire. MacKie has suggested that this episode may have been the result of attack by the Roman army during the early AD 140s. This is an attractive scenario although there is little positive evidence either to confirm or disprove it. MacKie cited the presence of a couple of large heat-fractured boulders which were of a different character to those found elsewhere in the broch: he suggested that these may have entered from above, as red-hot missiles launched by a Roman artillery engine to pierce and set light to the roof. There are, however, none of the more characteristic Roman artillery weapons, such as ballista bolts, which might be expected in MacKie's scenario. Whatever the story behind its destruction, some time later the site was re-occupied. The interior was largely cleared of rubble and parts of the wall were rebuilt to a height of around 3m. A succession of secondary

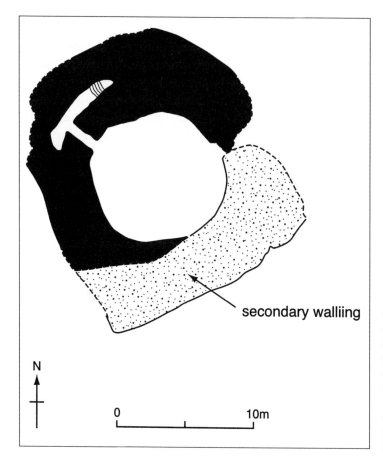

secondary walliing

N

0   10m

47 The southern broch of Leckie is an irregular structure which seems unlikely ever to have been of tower-like proportions. It most closely resembles some of the complex roundhouses of the west coast

hearths, still associated with Roman pottery, show domestic reuse in the second half of the second century AD.

The sudden destruction of the building, by whatever means it was achieved, led to the preservation of floor levels rich in artefactual debris. A scattering of rings, pins and brooches was found, as well as domestic equipment such as lamps and industrial fragments in the form of globules of lead. Roman objects were remarkably numerous, including a fine bronze mirror and Antonine pottery fragments. A series of iron spearheads and sword blades represent rare evidence for the presence of martial equipment within an Iron Age house. The finds from Leckie in general, however, support the sort of picture of Iron Age domestic and farming life suggested in chapter 4. There were the remains of iron shears for shearing sheep, the blade of a digging spade used for cultivating the soil (see **colour plate 21** for a comparable object from Lewis), stone weights from a loom, and a rotary quern used for grinding grain. The limited faunal evidence suggested a diet in which beef and mutton played a major role.

Buchlyvie

Further insights into the Forth Valley brochs were provided by Lorna Main's excavation of the Fairy Knowe at Buchlyvie, excavated from 1975-8. Prior to excavation, this was a largely featureless stony mound, badly disturbed by earlier road construction and wartime trenches, and set on a hillside on the southern edge of the carselands. The site gave extensive views over the river, 2km to the north, and, like Leckie, was well-sited for access both to the valley and to the rough grazings of the Gargunnock Hills.

Excavation revealed the remains of a poorly-preserved southern broch with an intra-mural chamber and guard cell, built over the remains of an earlier timber roundhouse. This earlier building seems to have been a substantial structure in its own right and may have been as big, if not bigger, than the broch itself. It belongs to a tradition of timber roundhouse building with a lengthy pedigree in southern and central Scotland (see chapter 2). The relationship of the broch to this earlier structure is intriguing. The timber roundhouse was certainly old, and may even have been abandoned, by the time the broch was constructed. Although the superstructure may still have been standing, the timber posts which supported its roof had rotted through at the base (the stumps of the posts were in fact recovered during the excavation). The broch was placed directly over the footprint of the earlier structure and the arc of its massive stone wall clearly followed the line of the older building. This suggests that the timber roundhouse was still visible when the broch was built. Perhaps then, the building of the broch simply represents the replacement of an existing high status (if rather decrepit) dwelling in a new architectural style.

Whatever the circumstances of its construction, the artefacts found within it suggest that the occupation of the broch may have been quite short-lived, perhaps no more than a generation or so. The occupation deposits at Buchlyvie yielded a wealth of artefactual material, much of it Roman in origin. Among the finds were fragments of Roman pottery, glass bottles and coins, all dating to the late first century AD. As at Leckie, Samian pottery was present in some profusion (at least 19 vessels were represented). Some of this pottery had clearly been reused after its initial breakage, since some bases had been cut off and smoothed down to make shallow plates, and other fragments had been reused as polishers or pigments. Other objects, while themselves not Roman, are redolent of Roman influence. A latch key of a type found on Roman sites was probably used to secure a chest or box of valuables (it is probably too small to be the 'front door key' of the broch), while lead weights and other objects were almost certainly made using metal obtained from the Roman army. Of the bronze-working debris from the site, around half seems to have incorporated Roman metal (the Roman alloys contain significant quantities of zinc which is present only in tiny levels in native alloys). Around 200 iron nails indicate that wooden fixtures and fittings within the broch were built using Roman-influenced carpentry techniques, since nails are virtually absent from native sites in Scotland before the Roman period. Stone bowls made from a type of stone found only in Argyll show that the inhabitants enjoyed trade relationships with distant native contacts, as well as with the Roman world.

In addition to a range of household objects showing evidence for leatherworking, wood-working and weaving, Buchlyvie produced some rare and important evidence for metal-working in both bronze and iron. Among the smithing tools was a set of iron compasses used to map out the complex curvilinear patterns associated with La Tène or 'Celtic' art. A corroded iron drawplate, used to shape metals such as bronze, iron, gold or silver into thin wire, was also found. A collection of bronze-working debris, which included an exceptionally large crucible, completes the picture of a bronze workshop which apparently had the capacity to produce large and highly decorated objects. There was also debris from iron working which showed a sophisticated mastery of blacksmithing techniques. Analysis showed that the iron was extremely 'clean', lacking the high levels of impurities such as slag and cinder, which commonly work their way into less well-produced iron objects. Given its seeming superiority over most native iron so far studied, it may be that this technology once again was the product of contact with Rome.

Several of the finds from Buchlyvie suggest the presence of high-ranking individuals. These include a finely worked enamelled finger ring, and gaming pieces of glass and stone, which seem, on analogy with gaming pieces elsewhere in Iron Age Britain, to have been restricted to the social élite. There were also parts of at least two spears, which, together with the weaponry from Leckie, support the interpretation that these southern broch-dwellers were involved in warfare, whether with their neighbours or with Rome. Warfare may in fact have been the cause of the broch's destruction as, like Leckie, it was burnt down and dismantled almost to its foundations. Since there was no sign of any post-Flavian material, it seems likely that this event occurred some time before the Antonine re-advance in the AD 140s.

As at Leckie, the inhabitants of Buchlyvie seem to have raised cattle, sheep and pigs. They also exploited a range of wild animals including red deer and wild boar. The occurrence of wild species is quite unusual for the period and it may be that the extensive wetlands of the Forth Valley sheltered a range of wild species which had disappeared in the face of over-hunting and intensive human land-use in other parts of the lowlands.

Broch neighbours

The biographies of Leckie and Buchlyvie, insofar as they can be reconstructed from excavation, show a range of striking similarities. Both were built in the late first century BC; Leckie during the Flavian period, and Buchlyvie either at the same time or slightly earlier. Both were clearly high-status buildings built by wealthy families, and both seem to have been built on existing timber roundhouse settlements. Both communities enjoyed extensive contacts with the Roman world and were able to obtain supplies of high quality Roman tableware and other desirable products. Both seem to have been burnt down, perhaps deliberately, although here their paths begin to diverge. Buchlyvie was probably abandoned (at least as a broch) some time before the Antonine re-advance, while Leckie was destroyed during or after that period. Both were subsequently re-occupied in modified form.

The other southern brochs within the Upper Forth Valley are less well understood, many having been excavated before the development of modern techniques. Nonetheless, it is likely that sites like Coldoch and Torwood would have had broadly similar histories of occupation to those revealed for Leckie and Buchlyvie. We should also bear in mind that there may be more of these structures still to be found. The Buchlyvie broch was only identified through the excavation of an unprepossessing stony mound, and there are many other such mounds in the area, not to mention the several 'duns' which may in some cases be simply less well-preserved brochs.

There is little doubt that the families who built and occupied these struc-tures would have been well known to each other, as relatives, neighbours, allies or perhaps rivals. There is little doubt, too, that the political disruptions caused by the fluctuations in Roman frontier policy would have pre-occupied these communities and caused considerable tension over the maintenance of land and power over several generations.

Copper lords of Berwickshire?

Perhaps the most visually impressive of the southern brochs is the site of Edin's Hall in Berwickshire (**48**), overlooking the Whiteadder Water, north of Duns. The imposing nature of the remains as they appear today is partly the product of the extensive antiquarian excavations of the late nineteenth century which removed the bulk of the internal deposits, leaving the walls of the broch and other structures clearly visible. At first glance the site bears a strong resem-blance to Gurness and the other Orcadian broch villages, as it forms the focal point of an enclosure filled with smaller buildings. Recent work on the site by Andrew Dunwell in the mid-1990s, however, has shown that Edin's Hall has a quite different history from that of Gurness, and that the superficial similari-ties between the two are probably quite misleading.

The site of Edin's Hall comprises three main elements: a hillfort, a broch, and a roundhouse settlement. The earliest detectable occupation takes the form of a hillfort, defined by two ramparts of stone and earth construction with external ditches. These have been badly disturbed by later occupation, but in places they have clearly been quite substantial. Indeed, even in their present reduced form they present a barrier some 4m high measuring from the base of the ditch to the crest of the rampart. Any internal buildings contemporary with

48 *The site of Edin's Hall in Berwickshire bears a superficial similarity to Gurness, but here the hillfort, internal buildings and broch represent a sequence of settlement activity built up over a considerable period of time*

this initial phase of settlement, however, have been entirely obscured by later occupation. Edin's Hall was one of many hillforts in the area, and there is little to suggest that it had any special status. Indeed a rather more impressive hillfort lies only around 1km to the south-west, on the summit of Cockburn Law. The chronology and function of southern Scottish hillforts is poorly understood, but one would expect that the construction and occupation of both sites would lie in the middle of the first millennium BC.

Somewhat later, the broch itself was constructed within a smaller enclosure inside the ramparts of the earlier hillfort. The broch was around 28m in diameter with a wall varying between 5-6m in thickness, nowhere more than 2m high (in fact the upper walling as seen today may be the result of restoration work carried out in the wake of the nineteenth-century excavations). In plan, the structure closely resembles the Atlantic roundhouses of the north and west: its narrow entrance passage has rebates for a timber door behind which lie two opposing guard cells; and three further cells lead off the central court, one of which gives access to an intra-mural stair. The interior of the broch at Edin's Hall, however, is exceptionally large. It measures around 18m in diameter, which is probably too great a distance ever to have been spanned by a single conical roof. Almost certainly then, it was never a tower-like structure comparable with the broch towers of the north and west.

The third major component of the site at Edin's Hall is the group of around 12 roundhouses, with accompanying enclosures and yards, which fills the remaining area within the hillfort defences, overspilling the decayed ramparts at several points. These range from as little as 3m to more than 14m in internal diameter and are of much slighter construction than the broch. A curving passage, reminiscent of the one at Gurness, leads through this sprawl of buildings from the eastern entrance, through the hillfort ramparts to the broch enclosure. Unlike the one at Gurness, however, the Edin's Hall passage is a composite feature incorporating different styles of walling at different points along its route. This seems to reflect the time-depth apparent within this collection of buildings, where certain walls clearly overlap or abut others. Although the removal of deposits during the early excavations makes it impossible now to reconstruct the original sequence of the buildings, it is clear that the 'village' accumulated piecemeal over time, rather than being a planned complex like its counterpart at Gurness. In fact the Edin's Hall buildings seem to form several discrete settlement units, each associated with a yard. At least two of these units have their own separate entrances independent of the long entrance passage.

The relationship between the broch and the outlying houses is open to several interpretations. Traditionally it had been thought that the broch came first, with the houses being constructed as the population and power of the settlement expanded. There are some problems with this, however. To begin with, the enclosure which separates the broch from the other houses abuts the wall of Structure 1, the largest of the outlying roundhouses. This implies that

Structure 1 was in place before the broch enclosure was built. Furthermore, the passage that leads to the broch is, as we have seen, a composite construction, and does not follow a straight course to the broch. Instead it skirts around Structure 1. This suggests that this roundhouse was already standing when the passage was built. So it may be the case that Structure 1, which although overshadowed by the broch was no mean structure in its own right (its internal diameter of more than 14m is greater than that of most Atlantic roundhouses), was the first large roundhouse on the site. Was it perhaps an exceptionally grand building constructed in the traditional vernacular style of the region? Later perhaps, when the wealth of the inhabitants had increased still further, was it displaced by the even more grandiose and exotic broch?

Unlike the other excavated southern brochs, Edin's Hall did not produce any Roman objects. At first glance, this might seem to suggest that the site had been abandoned prior to the Roman period. However, a fragment of a glass armlet found during the nineteenth-century excavations was almost certainly made from re-melted Roman glass, suggesting that there was at least some presence on the site during or after the Roman period. The most important finds from Edin's Hall, however, have a most unusual history. In 1976, a metal-detectorist reported finding a large ingot of copper in a field just 100m from Edin's Hall. This was claimed by the Crown as Treasure Trove and acquired by the National Museums of Scotland. At around the same time, another finder recorded the discovery of a second ingot, apparently from a different field around 150m from the site. During the course of the recent excavations, however, Andrew Dunwell was able to contact the finder of the first ingot who divulged the real circumstances of the discovery. Both ingots, it emerged, were found not only at the site of Edin's Hall itself, but actually within the broch. In fact they were located below the floor of the intra-mural cell at the foot of the stair. Since the monument had been in state care since 1887, any unauthorised metal-detecting or excavation at the site was obviously illegal, so the story of the original find-spots had been fabricated. The second ingot has now been lost, its last known owner having died some years ago. The first ingot, however, remains within the collections of the National Museums of Scotland.

The surviving Edin's Hall ingot has a composition of remarkably pure copper, suggesting that it is the product of primary smelting (rather than incorporating recycled metal). Since Edin's Hall lies just 1.4km from a series of disused copper mines at Hoardweel, it seems highly likely that the copper was a local product smelted either on the site or nearby. The surviving ingot weighs around 20kg and the lost one may have been similar, suggesting an original deposit of some 40kg of copper. This figure is quite remarkable, especially when one considers that high-status metal objects such as the bronze armlets characteristic of the Scottish Iron Age weigh only 0.8-1.8kg each, while a major piece like the Iron Age war trumpet known as the Deskford carnyx weighs only around 3kg. The Edin's Hall ingots clearly, therefore, represent a tremendous concentration of wealth. Their position, carefully secreted below the floor of a cell, may suggest burial for security, but in an Iron Age context may equally represent a foundation deposit or ritual offering to gods, perhaps to secure the continued productivity of the copper mines. In either case, there seems a strong probability that the wealth of the Edin's Hall community was built on their control of this rare and prized resource.

Politics, Rome and the southern brochs

Following his excavations at Torwoodlee in the early 1950s (**49**), Stuart Piggott developed a model which related the appearance of the southern brochs to the historically attested Roman incursions into southern Scotland. In essence, Piggott believed that the southern brochs were a single, unitary phenomenon associated with fluctuations in Roman frontier policy. Since he had identified Flavian pottery in deposits stratified below the walls of the Torwoodlee broch, Piggott reasoned that these structures had been built some time following the Agricolan withdrawal. The most likely scenario, in his view, was that rapacious northern broch-lords had moved southwards to fill the power vacuum created by the withdrawal of Roman forces from Scotland in the late AD 80s. Their ascendancy had lasted until the re-advance of the Roman army under

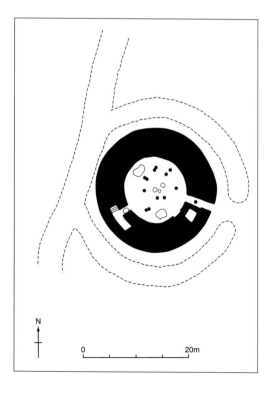

49 The southern broch of Torwoodlee in Selkirkshire, seen in this greatly simplified plan, was excavated by Stuart Piggott in the early 1950s. Like Edin's Hall it overlies the remains of an earlier hillfort. The ditch which runs around the base of the broch is joined to that of the earlier hillfort. The post-holes of a previous timber building can be seen in the interior, mirroring the situation at Leckie and Buchlyvie

N

0   20m

Antoninus Pius in the AD 140s, at which time the brochs were destroyed by the Roman army. At Torwoodlee, this episode was apparently marked by the partial demolition of the broch. The main reason for implicating the Roman army as the culprits was the presumption that any local aggressor would most likely have retained the broch for their own use rather than wilfully destroying it. In Piggott's scenario, the Roman material found on southern broch sites would have been acquired by looting abandoned Roman military installations.

Subsequent authors have also tried to relate the southern brochs to the ebb and flow of Roman frontier policy. Euan MacKie in particular has developed a model for the appearance of the southern brochs, which sees their relationship with Rome in a rather different light to that envisaged by Piggott. Rather than see the southern broch-builders as footloose northern freebooters, MacKie believes that they were allies of Rome, invited into southern Scotland at the time of the Roman withdrawal (in the late AD 80s) in order to help suppress native resistance. In MacKie's view, the quantity and quality of Roman material found on southern broch sites could only be the product of direct trade and could not have resulted from the looting of deserted forts. In this he is almost certainly correct. The decommissioning of Roman military installations was a painstaking business, as we can see from the excavations at Inchtuthil in Perthshire, where vast quantities of iron nails were carefully buried in pits to place them beyond native use. It seems hardly possible, therefore, that scavenging on abandoned forts could produce the type of high quality material found on southern broch sites. For MacKie, this suggests that the inhabitants of southern brochs enjoyed a favoured trading status with Rome which reflected their role as tiny 'buffer states' securing the peace in potential trouble-spots beyond the formal boundary of the Empire. Indeed, MacKie has gone further in developing this model, suggesting that these incomers may have been Orcadian chiefs whose association with Rome extended back to AD 43 and the Orcadian submission to Claudius discussed in chapter 5.

Like Piggott, MacKie sees the eventual destruction of the southern brochs as the outcome of renewed Rome aggression. While the Roman frontier was fixed on Hadrian's Wall far to the south, the Upper Forth Valley remained a distant bogland of little significance. The inhabitants of Leckie, Buchlyvie and their neighbours would have acted as useful allies securing the lands to the north of Empire. With the Antonine expansion of the early AD 140s, however, it became vital for Rome to secure unimpeded control over the main crossing point of the Forth at Stirling. The southern broch-dwellers had outlived their usefulness to Rome and were, accordingly, removed.

Despite differences of detail, MacKie's model is similar to Piggott's in several key respects. Both regard the southern brochs as products of warrior chiefs and their retinues moving in from the north, and both see the appearance and eventual destruction of the southern brochs as intimately bound up with the vagaries of Roman frontier policy. Both also see the southern brochs as defensive structures, which would have been perceived as a threat by the Roman army, rather than as essentially domestic buildings.

In recent years, there have been some challenges to these ideas. Firstly, the evidence for a northern origin seems rather difficult to sustain in detail. The southern brochs, for example, lack the sort of artefactual material, such as fine decorated native pottery, commonly associated with the Atlantic Scottish Iron Age. They are also a rather mixed bag in architectural terms. As we have seen, some like Edin's Hall seem too large to have ever been wholly roofed structures in the Atlantic roundhouse tradition. Could it be then that, rather than signalling the arrival of incoming northerners, the southern brochs might simply represent the importation of new architectural ideas? At several excavated southern brochs, such as Leckie and Torwoodlee, there is clear evidence for earlier occupation in timber buildings. At Buchlyvie, where the earlier occupation has been examined in the closest detail, this took the form of a substantial timber roundhouse, while at Edin's Hall there is some evidence to suggest that the broch succeeded a very substantial stone-walled round-house. It appears, therefore, that the best-known southern brochs were built on sites that were already associated with the local élite. Perhaps the adoption of elements of the Atlantic roundhouse architectural tradition reflects a further stage in the aggrandisement of communities who already enjoyed a high degree of prosperity and prestige. Northern influence is certainly clear, but northern incomers are perhaps less likely.

A second problem concerns the linkages which have been attempted between the adoption, use and destruction of the southern brochs and the historical sequence of events as it has been reconstructed from the limited documentary sources. The literary sources are themselves very fragmentary and should not be taken as a complete account of the political and military events of the period. In broad terms, however, if we wish to interpret the southern broch 'phenomenon' in the light of the Roman military incursions into Scotland, then we should presumably expect that each of these sites should have closely similar histories of construction, occupation and destruction. This, however, is not necessarily the case.

As we have already seen, Leckie and Buchlyvie can be dated quite closely by the presence of Roman material. Leckie seems to have been built during or after the Flavian period (the AD 80s) and was most probably burnt down in the Antonine period. Although Buchlyvie may have been built earlier, it is entirely possible that it too was constructed during the Flavian period. Older excavations of other southern brochs have also yielded Roman material, much of it of Antonine date. None of these provide sufficient chronological detail to give a precise chronology, although Torwoodlee yielded Flavian pottery from below the broch wall, showing that it, like Leckie, was probably built during or after the Flavian period. So far, so good. Unlike Leckie, however, Buchlyvie seems to have been destroyed and abandoned some time before the Antonine period. Furthermore, some sites have produced no Roman material at all. The absence of Roman finds from Edin's Hall is especially intriguing, as it lies well south of the Antonine Wall in an area which was at least periodically under direct Roman rule. Such an apparently high-status site would normally be expected to have had access to Roman goods. Their absence could suggest that Edin's Hall had either been abandoned or had undergone a significant decline in status some time before Agricola's legions first set foot in Scotland. While it is always dangerous to argue from the absence of evidence, it seems likely that there was no single chronological horizon of broch-building in southern Scotland, but perhaps a more gradual adoption of elements of broch architecture during the first century AD, i.e. before, during and after the initial Roman incursions. This lack of consistency in the chronological evidence is important because it serves to weaken the argument that sees the southern brochs as reflecting a single implantation of new peoples from the north. Yet if the southern brochs were not built by incoming northerners, then who did build them and why?

One answer may lie in the unstable social conditions of the late first century AD. The expanding Roman province to the south would inevitably have created tension and instability among southern Scottish communities even before Agricola's invasion. Opportunities for raiding, mercenary employment and slave-trading would have increased markedly as the Roman world came within closer geographical reach. In the background, there must have been concern over the steady expansion of imperial power, as southern allies and enemies alike lost their independence to Rome. Once Agricola began his campaigns in Scotland, the indigenous political structures of even the staunchest Roman allies would have been put under considerable strain. Many local élites would have experienced a considerable loss of both wealth and dignity as the army commandeered land for its forts, food to sustain its troops, timber for its massive building operations, and many other diverse resources. For the enemies of Rome, the picture would have been bleaker still. This would have been a period of opportunity for both advancement and disaster, and for those with wealth and power to protect, there would have been a good deal at stake. In such a time of flux, it is perhaps not surprising that new expressions of status and power began to emerge among indigenous communities. Lesley Macinnes, in her overview of the southern brochs, has suggested that broch architecture was adopted by those who were already rich and powerful, in order to reaffirm their status in a time of stress. It may even have been the very 'un-Roman', northern associations of broch architecture that made it attractive to southern élites, restating their native credentials in the face of Roman political domination. In such a fluid situation, each southern broch may have had a quite different history, reflecting the local experience of conflict and collaboration with the Roman world.

7

EPILOGUE

By the time southern brochs like Leckie and Torwoodlee were being built in the late first century AD, the Atlantic roundhouse tradition was already in terminal decline. Throughout the north and west of Scotland there were signs that communities no longer had the will or ability to construct new Atlantic roundhouses or to maintain long-established ones. At Clickhimin in Shetland, for example, the original broch tower was modified by the insertion of an inner wall casing (**50**), almost certainly built using stone removed from the upper walls of the building. This not only lowered the height of the building, but also greatly reduced its internal diameter so that it could be roofed using much shorter timbers. This suggests that the inhabitants may have been concerned both by the instability of the high tower and by the demands it placed on limited timber resources. Fragments of Roman glass from this secondary structure suggest that these modifications took place during the first century AD or perhaps even earlier. Elsewhere the picture is rather similar, for example at Dun Mor Vaul in Tiree, where Roman glass was found in deposits formed after the demolition of the broch tower.

Beyond the brochs

The passing of the Atlantic roundhouse tradition does not necessarily mean that the communities who built these great structures were themselves in decline. It may simply be that this particular form of monumental architecture, so costly to build and maintain, had ceased to be the prime means by which communities could display their status. There are various reasons why this might have happened. It may simply be that communities were no longer able to source the necessary timber to renew the roofs and floors of these buildings, or to provide sufficient fuel to heat the cavernous space enclosed by the roof. In all likelihood, however, timber and fuel were no more or less scarce in the early centuries AD than they had been in the last few centuries BC, and we

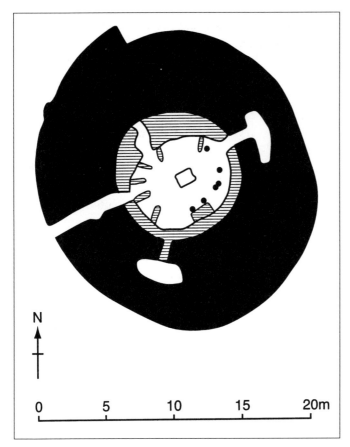

50 *Clickhimin: a simplified plan of the secondary roundhouse (note that this drawing does not indicate the outbuildings within the enclosure)*

probably need to seek a different explanation for the decline of the Atlantic roundhouse tradition.

One alternative suggestion relates to the different ways in which power and status might be displayed by societies at different levels of socio–political development. In a small-scale and fragmented society of the type which probably existed in the early part of the Iron Age, a major concern of individual communities would have been to secure control over the land and resources they required for survival. Outward displays of power and territoriality would most likely have been directed towards neighbouring communities. In such a society, monumental structures like Atlantic roundhouses might have served as symbols of the legitimacy of particular groups. Things began to change, however, in the last few centuries BC, with the emergence of larger and more complex settlements represented by broch villages like Gurness, Lingro and Howe. These were no longer made up of autonomous farming families, but instead seem to have comprised much larger agglomerations of population. As we saw in chapter 5, the leading families within these new societies may have held power well beyond the immediate locality. The power and influence of the most prominent individuals, like those based at Gurness, may at times have extended over much or perhaps all of Orkney, and possibly even further afield. What is important is that they exerted authority over people at a regional rather than local level; in other words, over people who were unlikely to visit the centres of power on any regular basis. While broch towers may have been an appropriate vehicle for display by prosperous farmers, jostling with each other for land and status, they may have been much less relevant for those whose ambitions extended to the carving out of regional kingdoms. Once effective control of local resources had been secured, the building and maintenance of Atlantic roundhouses may have been increasingly perceived as a costly and unnecessary indulgence.

Several of the Orcadian broch villages continued to flourish well into the first millennium AD. Gurness, for example, remained a thriving nucleated settlement into the second century AD and beyond, although the broch tower itself was progressively dismantled. Occupation of the smaller broch village at Howe seems also to have persisted until the middle of the first millennium AD, although the settlement underwent a steady decline from a nucleated village to a single farmstead. In both cases, however, the central broch towers had effectively disappeared from sight, if not from memory, long before the villages themselves were finally abandoned.

From broch to wheelhouse

In the Western Isles, too, Atlantic roundhouses probably ceased to be built by the end of the first millennium BC, although the detailed chronology for this area remains rather speculative. What is clear, however, is that a wholly new form of settlement became established as the standard architectural form for local farming families. These structures, known as wheelhouses, were characterised by a distinctive arrangement of internal stone piers bearing a vague resemblance to the spokes of a wheel (**51**). Each of the bays around the central area was capped by a corbelled stone roof and these were combined to form a ring of masonry around a central area roofed with timber and thatch.

Wheelhouses are found in great profusion in the Western Isles where they seem to represent a distinct settlement pattern which emerged in the last century or so BC and lasted perhaps into the second century AD. So far they have been found only in the Western Isles and Shetland, although the Shetland examples, as at Jarlshof and Old Scatness, are more solidly built and seem to be several centuries later in date. The absence of wheelhouses in Orkney is particularly striking given the substantial amount of archaeological work that has been carried out there.

Whereas the builders of Atlantic roundhouses had aimed to create an impression of height, strength and bulk, wheelhouses were all but hidden from view. Most were semi-subterranean, dug into sand hills or the ruins of earlier

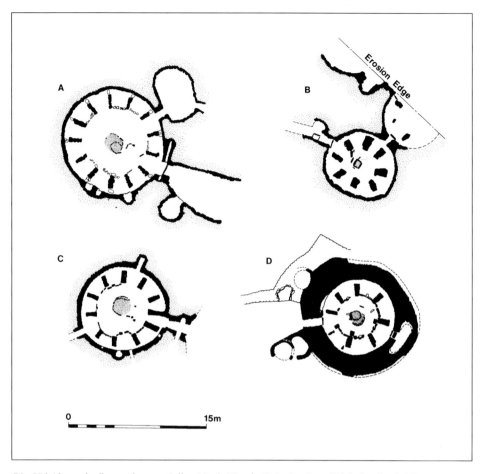

51 *Hebridean wheelhouse plans: a. Sollas, North Uist, b. Cnip, Lewis, c. Kilpheder, South Uist, d. Clettraval, North Uist*

buildings, with only their conical thatched roofs visible above ground level. Wheelhouses, however, offered considerable practical advantages over Atlantic roundhouses. The combination of stone and timber roofing meant that even fairly short timbers would have been quite sufficient to span the central area. Their semi-subterranean construction also provided good insulation and kept the roof low to the ground, protected from the Hebridean winds.

Yet wheelhouses were far from mundane functional dwellings. Even at Cnip in Lewis where there is one of the smallest wheelhouses known, the apex of the roof would have risen some 6m above the central hearth, while the stone piers would have arched upwards around the central zone to create an intricate and imposing internal space. Wheelhouses, like Atlantic roundhouses, were monumental buildings, but their monumentality was deployed to quite different effect. Rather than being projected outwards, the monumentality of wheelhouses was entirely inwardly directed so that it could be appreciated only by the inhabitants and their guests. It is tempting to suggest that the marked concern about access to land and resources which characterised the earlier period may have been largely resolved by the first century BC. This could have come about naturally, as established patterns of land-use, built up over generations of unbroken tenure, removed doubts and insecurities over the rights of particular communities to particular resources. Alternatively, it may have been externally imposed, perhaps reflecting the emergence of a higher level of authority with the power to grant and administer land rights.

Wheelhouse architecture was still employed for display and social competition, but perhaps now within a more integrated society where people gathered in one another's homes perhaps for feasting or general socialising; much like the ceilidhs of recent centuries. People may also have come together within these buildings for ritual activities. As we saw in chapter 4, several wheelhouses contain a range of unusual buried deposits, usually animal or human body parts placed in pits below the floor or behind the walls. The rituals associated with such deposits may have marked particular festivals or special times of year, or perhaps important happenings in the life of the community such as births, marriages and deaths.

The afterlife of brochs

By the time of the first Viking raids around AD 800, even the largest and most important broch villages like Gurness and Midhowe had long since been abandoned, grassed over and forgotten, except perhaps in story, myth and song. In Orkney, new centres of power had emerged, notably at the Brough of Birsay, and relatively slight, cellular houses had replaced the monumental architecture of earlier generations. During the course of the first millennium AD, Orkney, and perhaps other parts of Atlantic Scotland, had come under the authority of the expanding Pictish kingdom whose political centre of gravity lay across the sea, far to the south. A recorded 'destruction' of Orkney by the Pictish king Bridei, son of Bile, in AD 682 suggests, however, that the Pictish state's grip on the far north was never wholly secure and required periodic reassertion. It may partly have been this remoteness from the new centres of political and military authority that left the communities of Atlantic Scotland so exposed to Norse aggression.

The first Viking incursions were quickly followed by colonisation and political domination from Scandinavia. Norse control was soon extended to the Western Isles and Inner Hebrides, eventually absorbing most of the main areas in which Atlantic roundhouses had formerly been built. Although most Atlantic roundhouse sites had been long since reduced to grassy mounds or stony ruins, they nonetheless remained prominent places in the Pictish settlement landscape and it is likely that there would have been a host of myths and tales wound around them. As such, they seem to have been deemed suitable places for pagan burial. At least seven Viking graves were dug into the abandoned settlement mound at Gurness, for example, and Viking finds, probably from unrecorded burials, were regularly recovered in the early antiquarian excavations of broch sites in the north.

The occasional broch tower did of course still stand. The *Saga of Egil Skallagrimson* records how, around AD 900, an eloping couple spent a winter in 'Moseyarborg' (Mousa) while on their way from Norway to Iceland. Mousa appears once again in the *Orkneyinga Saga* in a rather similar episode from the twelfth century AD. This time Erlend the Young, having made off with Margaret, the Earl of Athol's widow, apparently held out in the ruins of the broch tower despite being besieged by the bride's disgruntled son, Harald, Earl of Orkney. The saga explains that Harald found it difficult to force his way into the stronghold, and that Erlend's advance preparations led to the eventual failure of the siege. Clearly Mousa at least was a well-known landmark during the Norse occupation of the Northern Isles and had acquired a reputation as a place of considerable strength. There are no records of the use of any other

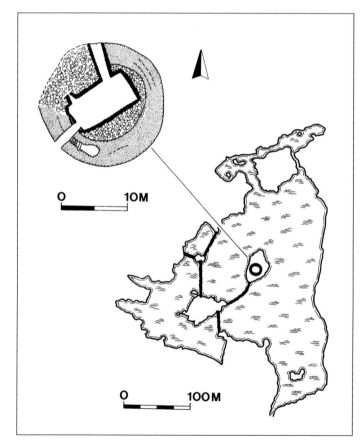

52 *The islet-sited broch tower of Dun an Sticer in North Uist was reused probably during the sixteenth century. A well-preserved rectilinear building was inserted into the ruins and the network of causeways was upgraded to accommodate wheeled vehicles*

53 *Excavations inside the Cnip wheelhouse, Lewis. The stone piers which divide up the interior were exceptionally well preserved*

broch towers at this time, however, and it seems likely that the extraordinary preservation of Mousa was a noteworthy exception to the rule even by the ninth century AD.

Sporadic reuse of ruined Atlantic roundhouses doubtless persisted throughout the succeeding centuries. Several sites in the Western Isles, for example, were re-occupied during the late medieval period, and there seem to be particular associations with the sixteenth century, a turbulent period following the collapse of the medieval Lordship of the Isles. In some cases, as at Dun an Sticer in North Uist, there are well-preserved remains of later buildings set within the earlier roundhouse (**52**). Elsewhere, local tradition relates the re-use of Dun Aonghas, also in North Uist, to the career of Aonghas Fhionn (Angus the Fair), whose activities may be reflected by traces of rectilinear buildings visible on the site today. A folk tale from Lewis, also believed to relate events from the sixteenth century, records how the Morisons of Ness hid out in the shell of Dun Carloway after raiding cattle from the local MacAulay clan. In hot pursuit, the local champion Donald Cam MacAulay scaled the outer wall and dropped burning bales of heather into the interior to smoke out the unfortunate Morisons. The implication seems to be that the walls of the broch tower were still more or less intact in the late medieval period, although we should perhaps bear in mind the attractive, if remote, possibility that the tale preserves a much older tradition of cattle-raiding and revenge.

FURTHER READING

A great deal has been written on the Atlantic Scottish Iron Age and this brief guide is intended to help the reader sift through this voluminous literature. The following sources deal with the Iron Age of Scotland in general terms:

Armit, I. 1997. *Celtic Scotland*. London: Batsford.

Armit, I. 1998. *Scotland's Hidden History*. Stroud: Tempus.

Edwards, K. & Ralston, I.B.M. (eds) 2003. *Scotland after the Ice Age: Environment, Archaeology and History, 8000 BC-AD 1000*. Edinburgh: Edinburgh University Press.

Ritchie, A. & Ritchie, J.N.G. 1981. *Scotland: Archaeology and Early History*. Edinburgh: Edinburgh University Press.

Books which cover the Atlantic Scottish Iron Age in more detail include:

Armit, I. (ed.) 1990. *Beyond the Brochs*. Edinburgh: Edinburgh University Press.

Armit, I. & Fojut, N. 1998. *Dùn Chàrlabhaigh and the Hebridean Iron Age*. Stornoway: Urras nan Tursachan.

Ritchie, J.N.G. 1988. *The Brochs of Scotland*. Aylesbury: Shire.

1 The broch hunters

Some of the key early texts referred to in the discussion of the history of research on brochs are:

Anderson, J. 1883. *Scotland in Pagan Times: the Iron Age*. Edinburgh: David Douglas.

Childe, V.G. 1935. *The Prehistory of Scotland*. London: Kegan Paul, Trench, Trubner & co.

Childe, V.G. 1946. *Scotland before the Scots*. London: Methuen.

Curle, A.O. 1927. 'The development and antiquity of the Scottish brochs'. *Antiquity* 1, 290-8.

Scott, W.L. 1947. 'The problem of the brochs'. *Proceedings of the Prehistory Society* 13, 1-37.

Descriptions of the history of research on brochs in the Western Isles, Orkney and Shetland respectively can be found in:

Armit, I. 1996. *The Archaeology of Skye and the Western Isles.* Edinburgh: Edinburgh University Press.

Fojut, N. 1998. 'How did we end up here? Shetland Iron Age studies to 1995', pp.1-42 in Nicholson, R.A. & Dockrill, S.J. (eds), *Old Scatness Broch, Shetland: Retrospect and Prospect.* Bradford: University of Bradford.

Hedges, J.W. 1985. 'The broch period', in Renfrew, A.C. (ed.), *The Prehistory of Orkney.* Edinburgh: Edinburgh University Press.

Some flavour of the debate between the diffusionist and anti-diffusionist camps in the 1960s-80s can be found in the following selection of papers:

Barrett, J.C. 1981. 'Aspects of the Iron Age in Atlantic Scotland. A case study in the problems of archaeological interpretation.' *Proceedings of the Society of Antiquaries of Scotland* 111, 205-19.

Clarke, D.V. 1970. 'Bone dice and the Scottish Iron Age.' *Proceedings of the Prehistoric Society* 36, 214-32.

Clarke, D.V. 1971. 'Small finds in the Atlantic Province: problems of approach.' *Scottish Archaeological Forum* 3, 22-54.

Lane, A. 1987. 'English migrants in the Hebrides: "Atlantic Second B" revisited.' *Proceedings of the Society of Antiquaries of Scotland* 117, 47-66.

MacKie, E.W. 1965. 'The origin and development of the broch and wheelhouse building cultures of the Scottish Iron Age.' *Proceedings of the Prehistoric Society* 31, 93-146.

MacKie, E.W. 1971. 'English migrants and Scottish brochs.' *Glasgow Archaeological Journal* 2, 39-71.

MacKie, E.W. 1983. 'Testing hypotheses about brochs.' *Scottish Archaeological Review* 2.2, 117-27.

Some classic excavation reports from before the 1980s:

Hamilton, J.R.C. 1956. *Excavations at Jarlshof.* Edinburgh: HMSO

Hamilton, J.R.C. 1968. *Excavations at Clickhimin.* Edinburgh: HMSO

MacKie, E.W. 1974. *Dun Mor Vaul: an Iron Age Broch on Tiree.* Glasgow: University of Glasgow Press.

The semi-broch controversy is covered in the following papers, with Harding providing a sceptical viewpoint:

Harding, D.W. 1984. 'The function and classification of brochs and duns', pp.206-20 in Miket, R. & Burgess, C. (eds) *Between and Beyond the Walls: Essays on the Prehistory and History of Northern Britain in Honour of George Jobey*. Edinburgh: Edinburgh University Press.

MacKie, E.W. 2000. 'Excavations at Dun Ardtreck, Skye, in 1964 and 1965.' *Proceedings of the Society of Antiquaries of Scotland* 130, 301–411.

MacKie, E.W. 1980. 'Dun an Ruigh Ruaidh, Loch Broom, Ross and Cromarty: excavations in 1968 and 1978.' *Glasgow Archaeological Journal* 7, 32–79.

2 From roundhouse to tower

Further information on the reconstruction of timber roundhouses can be found in the writings of Peter Reynolds, based on his work at Butser Farm, especially:

Reynolds, P.J. 1978. *Iron Age Farm: the Butser Experiment*. London: British Museum.

Reynolds, P.J. 1982. 'Substructure to superstructure', pp.173-98 in P.J. Drury (ed.), *Structural Reconstruction* (*British Archaeological Reports British Series* 110). Oxford: British Archaeological Reports.

The archaeological report on the excavations at Pimperne Down in Dorset, which formed the basis for much of this work is also worth reading, and includes sections on the reconstruction itself:

Harding, D.W., Blake, I.M. & Reynolds, P.J. 1993. *An Iron Age Settlement in Dorset: Excavation and Reconstruction* (Monograph Series No. 1). Edinburgh: University of Edinburgh, Department of Archaeology.

The hut circles of northern Scotland are best reviewed in the recent publication of the major excavation and survey programme at Achany Glen in Sutherland:

McCullagh, R.J. & Tipping, R. 1998. *The Lairg Project 1988-1996: the Evolution of an Archaeological Landscape in Northern Scotland*. Edinburgh: Scottish Trust for Archaeological Research.

The most up-to-date discussion of the Bronze Age cellular houses in the Northern Isles is contained in the recent excavation report on the multi-period site of Kebister in Shetland:

Owen, O. & Lowe, C. 1999. *Kebister: the four-thousand-year-old Story of one Shetland Township* (Society of Antiquaries of Scotland monograph no. 14). Edinburgh: Society of Antiquaries of Scotland.

For the archaeology of the early Atlantic roundhouses of the Northern Isles and north mainland, the most useful sources are:

Armit, I. 1990. 'Broch-building in northern Scotland: the context of innovation.' *World Archaeology* 21.3, 435-45.

Ballin Smith, B. 1994. *Howe: Four Millennia of Orkney Prehistory*, (Society of Antiquaries of Scotland monograph no. 9). Edinburgh: Society of Antiquaries of Scotland.

Fairhurst, H. 1984. *Excavations at Crosskirk Broch, Caithness* (Society of Antiquaries of Scotland monograph no. 3). Edinburgh: Society of Antiquaries of Scotland.

Hedges, J.W. 1987. *Bu, Gurness and the Brochs of Orkney, Part I: Bu* (British Archaeological Reports British Series 163). Oxford: British Archaeological Reports.

Mercer, R.J. 1985. *Archaeological Field Survey in Northern Scotland III, 1982-3*. Department of Archaeology, University of Edinburgh Occasional Paper 11, Edinburgh.

Renfrew, A.C. 1979. *Investigations in Orkney*. London: Society of Antiquaries of London.

A more general survey of the available dating evidence (though itself now rather outdated) is contained in:

Armit, I. 1991. 'The Atlantic Scottish Iron Age; five levels of chronology.' *Proceedings of the Society of Antiquaries of Scotland* 121, 181-214.

Some of the major Atlantic roundhouse sites recently excavated in the Western Isles are covered in the following publications:

Harding, D.W. & Dixon, T.N. 2001. *Dun Bharabhat, Cnip: an Iron Age Settlement in West Lewis, Volume 1, the Structures and Material Culture* (Calanais Research Series no. 2). Edinburgh: Department of Archaeology, University of Edinburgh.

Harding, D.W. & Gilmour, S.M.D. 2000. *The Iron Age Settlement at Beirgh, Riof Isle of Lewis, Volume 1, the Structures and Stratigraphy* (Calanais Research Series no. 1). Edinburgh: Department of Archaeology, University of Edinburgh.

The excavations at Dun Vulan in South Uist have proved to be fairly controversial and the excavators' claims regarding the date and original form of the monument have met with some opposition. This ongoing debate can be followed in the following publications:

Armit, I. 1997. 'Architecture and the household: a response to Sharples and Parker-Pearson', pp.266-70 in Gwilt, A. & Haselgrove, C. (eds) *Reconstructing Iron Age Societies: New Approaches to the British Iron Age*. Oxford: Oxbow Monograph 71.

Armit, I. 2000. 'Review of *Between Land and Sea: Excavations at Dun Vulan, South Uist* by Mike Parker Pearson & Niall Sharples.' *Antiquity* 74, 244-5.

Gilmour, S.M.D. & Cook, M. 1998. 'Excavations at Dun Vulan: a reinterpretation of the reappraised Iron Age.' *Antiquity* 72, 327-37.

Parker Pearson, M., Sharples, N.M. & Mulville, J. 1996. 'Brochs and Iron Age society – a reappraisal.' *Antiquity* 70, 57-67.

Parker Pearson, M., Sharples, N.M. & Mulville, J. 1999 'Excavations at Dun Vulan: a correction.' *Antiquity* 73, 149-52.

Parker Pearson, M. & Sharples, N.M. 1999. *Between Land and Sea: Excavations at Dun Vulan, South Uist*. Sheffield: Sheffield University Press.

Sharples, N.M. & Parker Pearson, M. 1997. 'Why were brochs built? Recent studies in the Iron Age of Atlantic Scotland', pp.254-265 in Gwilt, A. & Haselgrove, C. (eds) *Reconstructing Iron Age Societies: New Approaches to the British Iron Age*. Oxford: Oxbow Monograph 71.

3 Anatomy of a broch tower

Angus Graham's classic study remains the starting point for any analysis of broch architecture:

Graham, A. 1947. 'Some observations on the brochs.' *Proceedings of the Society of Antiquaries of Scotland* 81, 48-99.

More recent work on aspects of broch-building can be found in the following:

Fojut, N. 1981. 'Is Mousa a broch?' *Proceedings of the Society of Antiquaries of Scotland* 111, 220-8.

Hedges, J.W. 1987. *Bu, Gurness and the Brochs of Orkney, Part III: the Brochs of Orkney* (British Archaeological Reports British Series 163). Oxford: British Archaeological Reports.

Martlew, R. 1982. 'The typological study of the structures of the Scottish brochs.' *Proceedings of the Society of Antiquaries of Scotland* 112, 254-76.

A detailed consideration of timber usage in Atlantic Scotland, focusing on the collapsed and burnt timber roof from the secondary occupation at Dun Bharabhat can be found in:

Church, M. 2002. 'The archaeological and archaeobotanical implications of a destruction layer at Dun Bharabhat, Lewis', pp.67-76 in Ballin-Smith B. & Banks, I. (eds), *In the Shadow of the Brochs*. Stroud: Tempus.

More detail on the nature of Iron Age cosmologies, as reflected in architecture, can be found in the following papers:

Fitzpatrick, A.P. 1997. 'Everyday life in Iron Age Wessex', pp.73-86 in Gwilt, A. & Haselgrove, C. (eds) *Reconstructing Iron Age Societies: New Approaches to the British Iron Age*. Oxford: Oxbow Monograph.

Oswald, A. 1997. 'A doorway on the past: practical and mystic concerns in the orientation of roundhouse doorways', pp.87-95 in Gwilt, A. & Haselgrove, C. (eds) *Reconstructing Iron Age Societies: New Approaches to the British Iron Age*. Oxford: Oxbow Monograph.

Parker Pearson, M. & Sharples, N.M. 1999. *Between Land and Sea: Excavations at Dun Vulan, South Uist*. Sheffield: Sheffield University Press.

4 Broch landscapes, broch people

The best recent work on the Bronze Age settlement decline in the Scottish uplands is the monograph on the excavations at Lairg listed above under chapter 2. Detailed studies of the likely populations and territories associated with Atlantic roundhouses can be found in the following papers:

Fojut, N. 1982. 'Towards a geography of Shetland brochs.' *Glasgow Archaeological Journal* 9, 38-59.

Armit, I. 2002. 'Land and freedom: implications of Atlantic Scottish settlement patterns for Iron Age land-holding and social organisation', pp.15-26 in Ballin-Smith B. & Banks, I. (eds), *In the Shadow of the Brochs*. Stroud: Tempus.

A more detailed consideration of how social relationships and patterns of inheritance may have functioned has also been attempted:

Armit, I. in press. 'Land-holding and inheritance in the Atlantic Scottish Iron Age.' Turner, V. (ed.), *Tall stories: the Archaeology of Brochs*. Oxford: Oxbow.

Much of the information on crops, wild plants and other aspects of the economy of the Atlantic Scottish Iron Age has been collated in the following book:

Dickson, C. & Dickson, J. 2000. *Plants and People in Ancient Scotland*. Stroud: Tempus.

The most up-to-date consideration of the economic basis of the Atlantic Scottish Iron Age, although focusing on the post-broch period, is contained in the following papers:

Bond, J. 2002. 'Pictish pigs and Celtic cowboys: food and farming in the Atlantic Iron Age', pp.177-84 in Ballin-Smith B. & Banks, I. (eds), *In the Shadow of the Brochs*. Stroud: Tempus.

Dockrill, S.J. 2002. 'Brochs, economy and power', pp.153-62 in Ballin-Smith B. & Banks, I. (eds), *In the Shadow of the Brochs*. Stroud: Tempus.

The pottery associated with Atlantic roundhouses, especially in the west, is covered in the following recent papers:

Campbell, E. 2002. 'The Western Isles pottery sequence', pp.139-44 in Ballin-Smith B. & Banks, I. (eds), *In the Shadow of the Brochs*. Stroud: Tempus.

MacSween, A. 2002. 'Dun Beag and the role of pottery in the interpretation of the Hebridean Iron Age', pp.145-52 in Ballin-Smith B. & Banks, I. (eds), *In the Shadow of the Brochs*. Stroud: Tempus.

Reports on wheelhouse sites with evidence for ritual deposits can be found in the following excavation reports:

Barber, J., Halstead, P., James, H. & Lee, F. 1989. 'An unusual Iron
    Age burial at Hornish Point South Uist.' *Antiquity 63*, 773-8.
Campbell, E. 1991. 'Excavation of a wheelhouse and other iron age
    structures at Sollas, North Uist, by R.J.C. Atkinson in 1957.'
    Proceedings of the Society of Antiquaries of Scotland 121, 117-73.

5 Lords of the north

The report on the broch village at Howe has already been mentioned under chapter 2, and it is also a basic source for this chapter. The publication on Gurness by Hedges and lengthy rebuttals of the views of Hedges and others by Euan MacKie are as follows:

Hedges, J.W. 1987. *Bu, Gurness and the Brochs of Orkney, Part III:
    Gurness* (British Archaeological Reports British Series 163).
    Oxford: British Archaeological Reports.
MacKie, E.W. 1994. 'Gurness and Midhowe brochs in Orkney:
    some problems of misinterpretation.' *Archaeological Journal* 151,
    98-157.
MacKie, E.W. 1998. 'Continuity over three thousand years of northern
    prehistory: the "tel" at Howe, Orkney.' *Antiquaries Journal* 78, 1-42.

There is little literature on broch villages outside Orkney although the following reference is useful for Caithness:

Heald, A. & Jackson, A. 2001. 'Towards a new understanding of Iron
    Age Caithness.' *Proceedings of the Society of Antiquaries of Scotland*
    131, 129-48.

Surprisingly little has been written on the detailed interpretation of broch villages, but one interesting approach can be found in the following paper:

Foster, S.M. 1989. 'Analysis of spatial patterns in buildings (gamma
    analysis) as an insight into social structure: examples from the
    Scottish Atlantic Iron Age.' *Antiquity* 63, 40-50.

An examination of the degree of variation between regions in Atlantic Scotland at this time can be found in:

Armit, I. 1997. 'Cultural landscapes and identities: a case study in the
    Scottish Iron Age', pp.248-54 in Gwilt, A. & Haselgrove,
    C. (eds) *Reconstructing Iron Age Societies*. Oxford: Oxbow
    Monograph 71.

The following articles by Richard Hingley discuss some of the evidence for the reuse of Neolithic monuments in the Iron Age, while the book by Colin Renfrew details the excavations at Quanterness which, along with Howe, is one of the most relevant sites:

Hingley, R. 1996. 'Ancestors and identity in the later prehistory of Atlantic Scotland: the reuse and reinvention of Neolithic monuments and material culture.' *World Archaeology* 28(2), 231–43.

Hingley, R. 1999. 'The creation of later prehistoric landscapes and the context of the reuse of Neolithic and earlier Bronze Age monuments in Britain and Ireland', pp.233–51 in Bevan, B. (ed.) *Northern Exposure: Interpretative Devolution and the Iron Ages in Britain*. Leicester: Leicester Archaeology Monographs, No. 4.

Renfrew, A.C. 1979. *Investigations in Orkney*. London: Society of Antiquaries.

Andrew Fitzpatrick has provided a convincing reinterpretation of the relations between the inhabitants of Gurness and communities in southern England, while David Breeze's brief account sets the scene in terms of what the Roman army may have known of the geography of Scotland in the first two centuries AD:

Breeze, D.J. 2002. 'The ancient geography of Scotland', pp.11–14 in Ballin-Smith B. & Banks, I. (eds), *In the Shadow of the Brochs*. Stroud: Tempus.

Fitzpatrick, A.P. 1989. 'The submission of the Orkney Islands to Claudius: new evidence.' *Scottish Archaeological Review* 6, 24–33.

6 Towers in the south?

The following papers provide information on many of the southern brochs. Most are excavation reports dealing with individual sites, but the paper by Lesley Macinnes presents a more integrated overview:

Dunwell, A. 1999. 'Edin's Hall fort, broch and settlement, Berwickshire (Scottish Borders): recent fieldwork and new perceptions.' *Proceedings of the Society of Antiquaries of Scotland* 129, 303–57.

Macinnes, L. 1984. 'Brochs and Roman occupation of lowland Scotland.' *Proceedings of the Society of Antiquaries of Scotland* 114, 235–50.

MacKie, E.W. 1982. 'The Leckie broch, Stirlingshire: an interim report.' *Glasgow Archaeological Journal* 9, 60–72.

MacKie, E.W. 1987. 'Impact on the Scottish Iron Age of the discoveries at Leckie broch.' *Glasgow Archaeological Journal* 14, 1–18.

Main, L. 1998. 'Excavation of a timber round-house and broch at the Fairy Knowe, Buchlyvie, Stirlingshire, 1975-8.' *Proceedings of the Society of Antiquaries of Scotland* 128, 293-417.

Piggott, S. 1951. 'Excavations in the broch and hill-fort of Torwoodlee, Selkirkshire, 1950.' *Proceedings of the Society of Antiquaries of Scotland* 85, 92-117.

7 Epilogue

Little has been written specifically on the period when Atlantic roundhouses were in decline, but many of the excavation reports and general works cited above provide insights into this subject. The following sources deal with specific aspects of the period:

Armit, I. forthcoming. *Anatomy of an Iron Age Roundhouse: the Cnip Wheelhouse Excavations, Lewis.*

Batey, C. 2002. 'Viking and late Norse reuse of broch mounds in Caithness', pp.185-90 in Ballin-Smith B. & Banks, I. (eds), *In the Shadow of the Brochs*. Stroud: Tempus.

SITES TO VISIT

What follows is a small selection of the best-preserved Atlantic roundhouse sites, including most of the better known examples and a few personal favourites, listed alphabetically by region. For more detail on individual areas it is best to consult the various regional Inventories published over many years by the Royal Commission on the Ancient and Historical Monuments of Scotland (RCAHMS). These give detailed descriptions of individual sites and good snapshots of archaeological understanding at the time of publication. The series of regional guides, *Exploring Scotland's Heritage* (HMSO), provides good information on how to find the more visitor-friendly sites within each region.

Many of the sites listed below are in public ownership, a great many of them in the care of Historic Scotland. More information on these, for example regarding opening hours, can be obtained from Historic Scotland, Longmore House, Salisbury Place, Edinburgh, EH9 1SH. For those sites on private land, please always remember to ask permission before entering, be sure to close gates etc., and leave the site as you found it.

CAITHNESS AND SUTHERLAND

Dun Dornaigil, Sutherland
Historic Scotland
NGR: NC 457 450
This broch tower stands in a fairly remote location by the River Strathmore just south of Alltnacaillich, about 15 miles south of Hope on the A838. It is obvious from the road.

Carn Liath, Sutherland
Historic Scotland
NGR: NC 870 013
This site is easily visible from the A9 about 4km north of Golspie. A marked path leads to the site from the car park. The site lies within a stone-walled enclosure containing remains of several different periods, but some are probably contemporary with the central roundhouse.

LOWLAND SCOTLAND
Edin's Hall, Scottish Borders
Historic Scotland
NGR: NT 772 603
The site is signposted from the A6112. Cross the bridge at the bottom of the track and follow the signs across open ground along the side of the river. The walk takes at least 20 minutes.

ORKNEY
Gurness (Mainland)
Historic Scotland
NGR: HY 381 268
Follow the signs on the minor road that branches off the A966 between Finstown and Birsay.

Midhowe, Rousay
Historic Scotland
NGR: HY 371 305
From the ferry point to the mainland, head north-west along the B9064 for about 8km, then follow the signs along the footpath down to the coast.

SHETLAND
Mousa
Historic Scotland
NGR: HU 457 237
The island is reached by taking a small dedicated ferry. The broch tower is obvious on arrival, a few minutes walk along the shore from the pier.

Clickhimin (Mainland)
Historic Scotland
NGR: HU 464 408
The site lies on the outskirts of modern Lerwick, engulfed by modern housing estates. It is nonetheless well worth a visit.

Jarlshof (Mainland)
Historic Scotland
NGR: HU 399 095
The site lies near the southern tip of mainland Shetland, next to the Sumburgh Hotel, and is reached via the A970. A small visitor centre houses artefacts and displays covering the lengthy occupation of the site. As well as the Iron Age structures, there are extensive Viking remains.

Ness of Burgi (Mainland)
Historic Scotland
NGR: HU 388 084
Take the minor road along the Scatness peninsula as far as it goes, then carry on by foot for around 1km to the end. The narrow causeway to the site is potentially treacherous in wet or windy weather so take great care.

WESTERN ISLES
Dun Carloway, Lewis
Historic Scotland
NGR: NB 189 412
Dun Carloway (Chàrlabhaigh) stands just south of the modern township of the same name. The site is served by a small visitor centre and car park.

Loch na Beirgh, Lewis
NGR: NB 103 352
Although now reached across a boggy field, the site was originally an island linked by a substantial stone causeway to the adjacent high ground. When approaching along the minor road from the township of Riof, the road takes a sharp left just before reaching the beach of the Traigh na Beirgh. At the following sharp right turn, there is a gate to the field in which the broch tower lies.

Dun Bharabhat, Lewis
NGR: NB 098 353
The site occupies an islet in a small loch in the hills which form the interior of the Bhaltos peninsula. It is reached by ascending a narrow gorge from the rear of the Traigh na Beirgh. Follow the small stream with its succession of 'Norse' mills; at the top of the gorge turn left and walk around the loch. The causeway to the islet reaches the shore on the far side from the gorge. All in all, it is a short but testing walk.

Dun Vulan, South Uist
NGR: NF 714 298
The site occupies a spit of land between a sandy beach and a small loch on the west coast of South Uist. Turn west off the A865 at Bornish and follow the minor road to the beach.

WEST HIGHLANDS AND INNER HEBRIDES
Dun Beag, Skye
Historic Scotland
NGR: NG 339 386
The site occupies a prominent knoll just under 1km west of Bracadale.

Tirefour, Lismore
NGR: NM 867 429

The site occupies a commanding ridge with fine coastal views. It lies around 2.5km north-east of Achnacroish.

Dun Mor Vaul, Tiree
NGR: NM 042 492

The site occupies a rocky knoll around 400m north-west of the modern township of Vaul, around 4.5km north of Scarinish.

Dun Telve and Dun Troddan, Lochalsh
Historic Scotland
NGR: NG 829 172 and 834 172

Both broch towers are adjacent to the road through the narrow valley of Glen Beag, reached by following the minor road which leads south from Glenelg. Dun Telve is reached first, while Dun Troddan lies a few hundred metres further east.

Torr a' Chaisteal, Arran
Historic Scotland
NGR: NR 921 232

The track to this site is signposted from the A841. The roundhouse lies on a ridge overlooking the sea, about 500m from the main road.

INDEX